VANGUARD SERIES

EDITOR: MARTIN WINDROW

US 1st MARINE DIVISION 1941-45

Text by PHILIP KATCHER

Colour plates by MIKE CHAPPELL

OSPREY PUBLISHING LONDON

Published in 1979 by
Osprey Publishing Ltd
Member company of the George Philip Group
12–14 Long Acre, London WC2E 9LP
© Copyright 1979 Osprey Publishing Ltd
Reprinted 1986

This book is copyrighted under the Berne Convention. All rights reserved. Apart from any fair dealing for the purpose of private study, research, criticism or review, as permitted under the Copyright Act, 1956, no part of this publication may be reproduced, stored in a retrieval system, or transmitted in any form or by any means, electronic, electrical, chemical, mechanical, optical, photocopying, recording or otherwise, without the prior permission of the copyright owner. Enquiries should be addressed to the Publishers.

ISBN 0 85045 311 9

Filmset by BAS Printers Limited,
Over Wallop, Hampshire
Printed in Hong Kong

Cover illustration
Mike Chappell's cover painting shows men of the 1st Marine Division advancing through the elephant grass of Cape Gloucester in December 1943, supported by a cast-hull M4A1 Sherman tank of the 1st USMC Tank Battalion. It is taken from a photograph, and shows the very plain appearance of tanks of the divisional battalion—all markings, including national stars, are omitted except for small white vehicle numbers on the front and rear quarters of the turret. The printed camouflage combat suit was not much used in the 1st Division, according to photographic evidence; we have included it here for interest, but in fact the normal OD fatigues seem to have been the norm at Cape Gloucester.

Marines man a 40mm anti-aircraft emplacement (note range-finder on right) overlooking the beaches of Guadalcanal. (This, and all other photographs, courtesy of US Marine Corps)

Before the Battle

On 1 February 1941 the First Brigade of the US Marine Corps, which had been formed to test the latest ideas on amphibious warfare, became the First Marine Division. Already known in the corps as 'the raggedy-ass Marines' because of their tough assignments, the new First Division continued its rugged training schedule. 'We never really came out of the boondocks from then on,' a Division veteran later recalled, 'from the fall of 1940 when the brigade went to Guantanamo (Cuba) until after it had, as the First Division, secured Guadalcanal.'

Spring 1941 found the Division involved in the largest American exercise of its kind, a mass landing off New River, North Carolina. When the exercise ended, most participants returned to comfortable bases—but not the First. They went into 'tent city' at the brand-new Camp Lejune, North Carolina. There they continued their training in jungle terrain surprisingly similar to that of the yet-unknown island of Guadalcanal. Pearl Harbor, 7 December 1941, found the Division with a strength of only 518 officers and 6,817 enlisted men, but the Japanese sneak attack brought in a wave of volunteers.

In late March 1942 the Division received orders

for overseas duty. The 7th Marines—a Marine Corps regiments is called a 'Marine'—left Norfolk, Virginia on 10 April, reaching Apia, Western Samoa on 8 May. They stayed for five months on defensive duty. The rest of the Division went to Wellington, New Zealand.

The 1st Marines and supporting units had to go by rail to San Francisco, California, to be shipped out, while the 5th Marines and Division artillery (Divarty) left Norfolk on 10 May 1942 on the *Wakefield*, an old passenger liner. 'A few of us shared the terrible truth that life jackets and life boats existed for less than half our numbers,' Division Commanding General A. A. Vandegrift wrote later. 'Fortunately enemy and weather co-operated to provide an uneventful if tiresome trip, broken only on the last lap. Due to intense heat we were sailing with hatches open despite a heavy sea. Suddenly the old girl struck a monstrous swell that sent tons of water below deck. For a moment I feared panic, but some unknown hero broke the tension by yelling, "Women and children first!"'

In 1942 a **US Marine Division** included the following basic combat units:

Three infantry regiments, each of three battalions, each of approx. 1,000 men
One artillery regiment, of four battalions, fielding
    12 × 155mm
    12 × 105mm
    36 × 75mm guns
One engineer regiment of approx. 2,500 men
One tank battalion initially equipped with M3 Stuart tanks
One US Navy Coast Defence battalion
Support units totalling some 2,600 men.

The exact composition of the 1st Marine Division at various stages of its service in the Second World War will be found listed at the end of the main narrative text.

The Division's new camp was on North Island, some thirty-five miles from Wellington. Staff officers moved into the Hotel Cecil in downtown Wellington. The Division had never been posted so close to a city the size of Wellington before, and the men took advantage of the city's delights and the friendly inhabitants. One day General Vandegrift met 'an elderly, stern-looking gentleman with a clipped white moustache.' The old man wanted to know if he was the general commanding the Division. He was, the general said. The old man then said, 'Well, sir, I am very glad to meet you. I want you to know, sir, that I have lived at the Hotel Cecil for twenty-six years.' General Vandegrift, knowing how the residents were evicted to make room for his officers, braced himself for a blast. 'I want you to know, sir,' the old gentleman went on, 'how pleased I am to move from my apartment so that you and your officers have a place to do your job.' Afterwards the general wondered how many people in other countries would have been so pleasant about their enforced moves.

Another meeting the general had was less pleasing. Vice-Admiral Ghormley, South Pacific Area commander, met General Vandegrift on 26 June 1942 in Auckland. He told the general that the Division was to 'Occupy and defend Tulagi and adjacent positions (Guadalcanal and Florida Islands and the Santa Cruz Islands) in order to deny these areas to the enemy and to provide United States bases in preparation for further offensive action.' When was this to take place, the general asked. 'D-Day will be 1 August,' replied the admiral.

The Division's second echelon was not due until 11 July. Not all the Division's equipment was 'combat-loaded,' so that it could be brought ashore first with items needed for combat. The Division had less than a month to unload all its equipment and reload it combat style. Even though the actual date of 'D-Day' was later pushed back to 7 August, it still took around-the-clock work to unload and reload ships. On 31 July the Division pushed off for Guadalcanal with 956 officers and 18,146 enlisted men. It was only after they were aboard and under way that the men learned their destination, and final plans were made.

'This is going to be a difficult matter,' one lieutenant-colonel commanding troops going in on the first wave said at their final briefing, 'with rivers to cross, the grass four to five feet tall, and the drainage ditches. . . . But it can be done, and it must be done, and we've got to lead the way.'

A sand-bagged 75mm pack howitzer position on the coast of Guadalcanal.

Guadalcanal

The important thing about Guadalcanal was not so much the taking and holding of an airfield, important though that may have been. It was that for the first time Americans attacked and beat Japanese. The spell of defeats at Wake Island and the Philippines, Pearl Harbor and Indonesia was broken. Guadalcanal proved that the Japanese could be and eventually would be beaten.

Guadalcanal itself was an accidental battle. Nobody would have chosen to fight there. Jack London, who described the lush, densely jungled island as a malaria-ridden 'place of death,' wrote, 'If I were a king the worst punishment I could inflict on my enemies would be to banish them to the Solomons.' The islands were Japan's southernmost outposts. Previous conquerors had been smart enough to avoid living on Guadalcanal. By the time of the invasion the only civilian inhabitants were in several Catholic missions, a few coconut plantations and a Burns-Philp trading station. The island's main population comprised giant lizards, scorpions, crocodiles, poisonous spiders, leeches and ferocious white ants.

These elements made up the bulk of the defending force that met the Marines when they landed. Instead of putting up the fierce defence expected, the few Japanese in the landing areas fled on spotting the Marines. At 9.08am on 7 August, the boats carrying the 1st and 3rd Battalions of the 5th Marines (hereafter written as 1/5th Marines and 3/5th Marines), bore away for shore. Two minutes later the battalions hit the beach, landing abreast with the 1/5th Marines on the right. At 11am the 1st Marines (reinforced) landed behind the two battalions and all units began moving towards a hill described as 'the grassy knoll' by a British planter before the invasion.

It was the terrain rather than the Japanese which slowed down the Marine advance. General Vandegrift, accompanied by a corporal armed with a 12-gauge shotgun, landed shortly after the assault troops and looked over their advance. 'On the beach west of the main perimeter I found the 1st Battalion, 5th Marines, moving as if it were about to encounter the entire Imperial army. I gave the battalion commander hell . . . the day's objective was the Tenaru [actually, the Ilu] river, about two miles west, which I wanted defended by nightfall.

'At Cates' CP I learned that his right battalion was bogged down in an immense rain forest west of the Ilu [actually, the Tenaru] river. Our informants in New Zealand had failed to report this obstacle, a foetid morass so thick with overgrowth you couldn't see Mt Austen or anything else from its depths. In working their way through it the troops, in poor condition from the weeks aboard ship, seemed about done in by the heat and high humidity.'

American planners, working with very old maps and verbal information from planters and visitors, had incorrectly labelled the Ilu River the Tenaru and vice versa. This not only confused them then, but has confused historians ever since, with some accounts using period designations and others (such as this one!) the correct names.

While landings on Guadalcanal itself were unopposed save by nature, simultaneous landings within the island chain were meeting with stiff opposition.

The 1st Marine Raider Battalion was sent to the island of Tulagi, the capital of the British Solomon Islands Protectorate, on the Florida side of the chain. The battalion, under tough Lieutenant-Colonel Merritt E. 'Red Mike' Edson, landed its 'B' and 'D' Companies at 8am on the western end of the roughly rectangular island. The spot was chosen in the hope that it would be undefended.

Such was the case, and a signal went out at 8.15, 'Landing successful, no opposition.' Quickly the 2/5th Marines, under Lieutenant-Colonel Harold E. Rosecrans, landed behind the Raiders and turned north-west while the Raiders headed south-east. The north-west was quickly covered without meeting any Japanese, and the 2/5th Marines then returned to support Edson's troops.

The Marines met their first resistance in the small town around the Burns-Philp docks on the north end of the island. There the Marines halted after taking over three-quarters of the island, along a ridge running between a wharf on the north and the Residency buildings towards the south. The men dug themselves shallow two- and three-man foxholes for the night.

It was the night the Japanese were waiting for. According to one of their training manuals, 'Westerners—being very haughty, effeminate and cowardly—intensely dislike fighting in the rain or mist or in the dark. They cannot conceive night to be a proper time for battle—though it is excellent for dancing. In these weaknesses lie our great opportunity.'

The Raider companies were in line, reading from the north, 'B', 'D', 'A' and 'C'. The Japanese, under cover of darkness and mortar fire,

Marines wade across the Lunga river at the start of a dusk patrol.

hit between Companies 'A' and 'D', cutting through and then turning on 'A'. The company held on, turning back four different attacks. One of those who stopped the Japanese was Private First Class John Ahrens. Next morning he was found, still clutching his Browning Automatic Rifle, his green fatigues splashed black with his own blood which oozed out of five wounds in his chest, two from bullets and three from bayonets. A dead Japanese officer lay across his legs and a sergeant next to him. Some thirteen more dead Japanese littered the ground in front of his foxhole. Captain Lewis W. Walt, Co. 'A' commander, gathered the slowly breathing Ahrens in his arms. 'Captain,' the dying man whispered, 'they tried to come over me last night, but I don't think they made it.' The captain picked him up to take him to the Residency to die. 'They didn't, Johnny,' he said softly, 'they didn't.'

The attacks had cost the Japanese dearly and they could make only token opposition as the next morning the 2/5th Marines pushed passed the Raiders, taking the last part of the island by 3pm. The pattern for Pacific battles had been set.

Another large island in the chain was Florida, which fell to Co. 'B', 2nd Marines without opposition. Tiny Gavutu, a speck some 300 yards

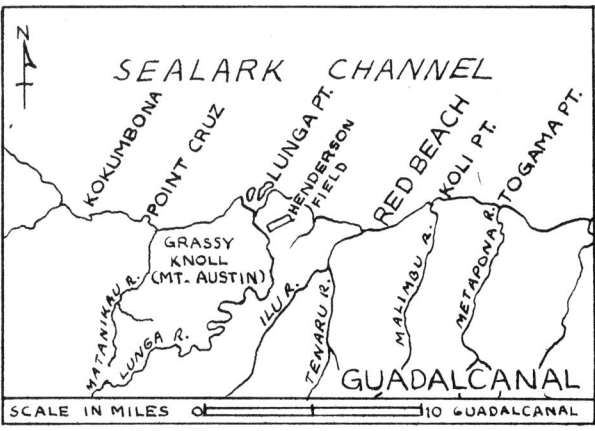

wide and 500 yards long, was a tough nut to crack, however. The Parachute Battalion landed there from boats, under covering fire from destroyers, at about noon on 7 August. The naval fire broke up Japanese seaplane ramps, so several boats detoured to land by a nearby concrete dock. As they hit the beaches, covering fire ceased and the well-dug-in Japanese opened up. The battalion commander was hit almost as soon as he landed. One out of every ten men who made it to the dock was wounded and the whole right flank was pinned down on the narrow beach. It was not until 2pm that a squad took the highest point on the island, Hill 148. Even so, the troops could not move off the island to take the nearby and equally small Tanambogo since so many Japanese remained on Gavutu hidden in caves and pillboxes.

While Marines went about the island tossing explosive charges into these caves, at 6.45pm Co. 'B', 2nd Marines tried to cross the narrow strait to Tanambogo. Flares exposed them to enemy fire when still in the water, and they had to fall back. The night brought constant attacks from individual Japanese who crawled out of their caves to toss grenades into Marines' foxholes. The next day Lieutenant-Colonel Robert G. Hunt's 3/2nd Marines successfully landed on Tanambogo with two tanks. The Japanese stopped one of the tanks by jamming a bar into its treads, and then covered it with Molotov cocktails. One Marine threw open the turret hatch and jumped out. Rolling off the turret, he landed in a shallow hole only to be rushed by Japanese. Infantrymen began picking off the Japanese one by one, and eventually the tanker got back to safety.

7

The three islands around Guadalcanal—Tulagi, Gavutu and Tanambogo—had been garrisoned by some 1,500 Japanese. Of these, twenty-five were captured alive and some seventy were thought to have escaped to other islands. The rest were dead—a grim indication of what the Marines could expect in the future.

On Guadalcanal proper the enemy had not yet been seen in any large numbers. Fleeing Japanese abandoned, on their airfield, two generators, machine shops, an air-compressor factory for torpedoes and even an ice plant, which the Marines quickly decorated with a sign: 'Tojo Ice Plant, Under New Management.' By the 9th the airfield, named 'Henderson Field' after Major Lofton R. Henderson, a Marine flyer killed at Midway, was firmly held by Marines. A defensive perimeter some 9,600 yards long was set up, with the Divarty's 75mm and 105mm howitzers in its centre. On 20 August two squadrons, one of fighters and the other of dive bombers, landed at Henderson Field to make it their base.

Things were not all that good, however. The US Navy was obliged by plane losses and petrol shortages to withdraw the supporting ships. Except for the two air squadrons, the Division was on its own.

At first, the Japanese 17th Army, under Lieutenant-General Harukichi Myakutake, did not realize the potential threat of Henderson Field. Considering the Marines there to be simply

Lt.-Gen. Thomas A. Holcomb, Col. Merritt A. Edson of the Raider Bn., and 1st Division commander Maj.-Gen. Alexander A. Vandegrift confer during Gen. Holcomb's inspection of Guadalcanal.

a nuisance, they sent a force of some 6,000 men under General Kiyotake Kawaguchi to retake the island. General Kawaguchi, who told a reporter that the attack would be 'extremely serious business', had his men paid and well fed to put them in good heart for the fight. Then, just before midnight on 18 August the advance party of Colonel Kiyono Ichiki and 915 men of the 28th Infantry Regiment landed on Guadalcanal. Leaving some 125 men to hold the beachhead, Colonel Ichiki's force pushed towards the dug-in Marines.

At about 1.15am on 21 August, Colonel Ichiki's force was facing 2/1st Marines dug in along the Ilu river. A green flare was the signal for a *banzai* attack. A Marine guard fired a single shot towards the flare, and then the Japanese came splashing across the green scum of that stagnant creek. Private Robert Leckie was one of the defenders:

'Everyone was firing, every weapon was sounding voice; but this was no orchestration, no terribly beautiful symphony of death, as decadent rear-echelon observers write. Here was cacophony; here was dissonance; here was wildness; here was that absence of rhythm, the loss of limit, for everyone fires what, when and where he chooses; here was booming, sounding, shrieking, wailing, hissing, crashing, shaking, gibbering noise. Here was hell.'

One Marine machine gunner nicknamed 'The Indian' was caught by a burst from a Japanese machine gun and died, his finger pressed to the trigger, his weapon coughing out bullets as his dead body leaned into it. In death he fired two

A patrol heads up the Ilu, in search of two troublesome Japanese 77mm field guns.

hundred more rounds into the oncoming Japanese.

Private Al Schmidt, wounded in the leg, the rest of his crew dead about him, kept loading and firing his machine gun across the unmoving stream. Finally one Japanese tossed a hand grenade into his foxhole, the flying fragments blinding him and tearing into his arms and shoulder. 'I can smell the rotten buggers', he yelled, and kept on firing. When fellow Marines finally got to him, he'd been firing steadily for over five hours. Private Schmidt was awarded the Medal of Honor.

About 2.30am the reserve platoon of Co. 'G' went into action. An artillery barrage was called in on the persistent Japanese at about 3am. M3 Stuart tanks from Co. 'B', 1st Tank Battalion, fired cannister from their 37mm guns into the Japanese infantry, then drove forward, crushing Japanese hiding in the shrubbery. Ordered to return, the tank commander declined with the words, 'Leave us alone—we're too busy killing Japs!' At about 8.30am the 1/1st Marines came up, and by then the Japanese knew it was all over. Pinned against the sea, some 250 survivors tried to escape along the beach at about 2pm, only to be hit by waiting fighters from Henderson Field. The Marines took only fifteen prisoners, thirteen of whom were wounded. Virtually all the rest were dead. Total Marine losses were thirty-four killed and seventy-five wounded.

'The attack of the Ichiki detachment', Tokyo was informed, 'was not entirely successful.'

On 21 August the 2/5th Marines were brought from Tulagi to form a mobile reserve for the Guadalcanal garrison.

The Japanese realized that their error lay in underestimating US strength on Guadalcanal, and so sent General Kawaguchi's 35th Brigade of some 2,400 men to Taivu Point, while Colonel Akinsouke Oka's 1,100 men landed at Kokumbona, ten miles west of the airfield. The plan called for a joint attack.

Officers in the 35th Brigade, white crosses painted on their backs for quick identification, led an attack against the main position due south of the field along a high point thereafter known as 'Bloody Ridge'. At about 9.30pm they ran into

Men of the 7th Marines take a break during the advance on the Mataniko. Note details of dress and equipment, and the grenade pouch rig worn by the man in the middleground.

A heavy 155mm howitzer in position on Guadalcanal.

Co. 'C', Marine Raiders, driving a whole platoon back against the Lungga. Company 'C' fell back, joined by Co. 'B', but the rough terrain kept the Japanese from taking advantage of their victory.

The next day the 2/5th Marines were sent to support Colonel Edson's Raiders, despite his protests that the Raiders alone could hold the ridge. Most of the 2nd Battalion never got to the ridge, held up by rough terrain and Japanese air attacks. New defensive lines were dug around the southern slope of the high knob in the centre of the ridge.

As daylight faded away, the noise from the Japanese lines increased. A smoke pot was rolled into Marine lines with the yell 'Gas attack', probably from an English-speaking Japanese. Finally the Japanese, screaming and firing their weapons from their hips, came on. 'The attack was almost constant,' wrote 2/5th commander Major William McKennon, 'like a rain that subsides for a moment and then pours the harder. In most of these assaults the Japs never reached our lines ... When one wave was mowed down—and I mean mowed down—another followed it into death. Some of the Jap rushes carried them into our positions and there was ugly hand-to-hand fighting. But not one of our men, to my knowledge, met death that night by a Jap bayonet.'

The whole line slowly fell back under Japanese pressure, re-forming along what had been the battalion reserve line, while 105mm howitzers opened up in support. By dawn it was all over. Another Japanese attack 'was not entirely successful.'

Colonel Edson and one of his company commanders were awarded Medals of Honor for their night's work. General Kawaguchi reported 633 men dead and 505 wounded. The survivors, beaten and starving, made their way to Colonel Oka's position. For the moment the Japanese had been stopped.

At this point General Vandegrift felt strong enough to begin offensive operations. On 23 September the 1/7th Marines were sent to cross the Mataniko and scout the hilly country beyond that river. Quickly they ran into some Japanese, and 2/5th Marines were sent as reinforcements. By the 26th the two battalions still had not crossed the Mataniko, and the Raiders were sent up to attempt the crossing. It took three separate attempts to gain a foothold on the western side of the river, with the Marines taking more casualties than in any other part of the campaign, but by 9 October they were across and their lines had been advanced three miles.

The Japanese were still not ready to give up Guadalcanal. Lieutenant-General Masao Maruyama, 2nd Division, told his men: 'This is the decisive battle between Japan and the United States, a battle in which the rise or fall of the Japanese Empire will be decided.'

On 11 October the Japanese reinforced their troops with artillery, and on 13 October they laid down a huge naval bombardment on Henderson Field. The bombardment, which began at about 1.30am, included 14-inch shells from the battleships *Harunga* and *Kongo* and eight- and five-inch shells from supporting vessels. The shelling lasted until about 3am, leaving hundreds of men more battered and shocked by the pure intensity of it than by its actual ballistic effects.

By 19 October, the 2nd (*Sendai*) Division, two battalions of the 38th Division, three batteries of heavy artillery, a battery of mountain artillery, a mortar battalion, three rapid-fire gun battalions and a force of sixteen tanks were ashore, totalling some 20,000 men. Combining these with the remains of the first two forces, the Japanese finally outnumbered the Americans. The First Marine

Division itself had received reinforcements in the shape of the 164th Infantry Regiment, an Army National Guard outfit.

The Japanese plan this time was elaborate. Their 4th and 124th Regiments, with heavy artillery and tanks, were to hit positions on the lower Mataniko, then push towards Henderson Field. The 16th and 29th Regiments would go by them and, following an artillery barrage, attack the southern perimeter. The lower Mataniko attack was one of several scheduled to hit at the same time. Another would fall on the upper Mataniko, while a third would hit Bloody Ridge. Unfortunately for the Japanese, their heavily loaded troops failed to get into position for their assigned attacks by 'D-Day' on 22 October. Their commanders did not know this, however, because of poor communications.

At 6pm on 22 October, Japanese artillery opened up on the lower Mataniko positions held by the 1/7th Marines and a battalion of the 164th. Following the barrage the Japanese infantry charged, led by nine 18-ton tanks. Marine anti-tank fire stopped all but one tank, which rolled over the American foxholes until a Marine jammed a hand grenade in its tracks. With that the tank rocked back and forth once, and a tank destroyer caught it in its sights. A lucky shot, which must have hit its ammunition supply, blew the tank twenty yards back into the sea. The attack was stopped.

After that attempt had been beaten off, General Vandegrift reasoned that the main attack would fall on the upper Mataniko. The 2/7th Marines were sent to reinforce the 3/7th Marines already there. This left Lieutenant-Colonel Lewis 'Chesty' Puller's 1/7th Marines as the only force holding Bloody Ridge. At about 3am on 24 October the next Japanese attack was launched, hitting the 1/7th on the ridge. By 3.30 the 164th's reserve battalion was sent in as reinforcements. Even though they went into strange positions, under fire and at night, the Army troops acquitted themselves well. It was the Marines who had to take the main weight of the defence, however. Sergeant John Basilone, who earned the Medal of Honor that night, said later, 'They kept coming and we kept firing. We all thought our end had come.' The attack was a typical *banzai* charge, notable for a lack of tactical subtlety. When the rushes finally stopped, at around 7am, the Marines and soldiers counted 941 bodies under their guns.

The attack on the upper Mataniko finally came on 25 October, hitting Companies 'F', 'G' and 'E', 7th Marines. The weight of these charges virtually wiped out Co. 'F' and pushed back Co. 'E'. Linking those two companies was a machine-gun platoon led by Sergeant Mitchell Paige, whose fight here earned him a Medal of Honor and a battlefield commission as second lieutenant. Paige not only did not pull back, but actually led his men forward, cradling his .50 calibre water-cooled machine gun in his arms and firing as he went. When the fight was over some 110 dead Japanese lay in front of his position.

The overall Japanese plan, cursed by over-optimism and faulty intelligence, had failed.

What the Japanese couldn't do, Guadalcanal's terrible environment could. The Division reported 1,941 malaria cases in October alone. Even those men who were physically well enough, if a bit thin, were mentally deadly weary. They had been putting up with rougher conditions than most Marines plan to endure for any length of time.

One thing which could be done for morale would be a return to the offensive. On 1 November General Vandegrift launched an attack across the Mataniko. The 1/5th Marines were stalled for a time on the right, but 2/5th Marines moved ahead smartly on the left. The reserve battalion, 3/5th Marines, went into line with 1/5th Marines on 2

(Left) Admiral William F. 'Bull' Halsey, commanding officer in the South Pacific, with Gen. Vandegrift (centre) during an inspection tour of the Guadalcanal positions. Note sun helmets with USMC insignia worn by Vandegrift and his aide on the right.

Interesting photo of new M4 Sherman tanks making practice landings from an LCT outside the reef of Rua Sura Island, near Guadalcanal. The original print shows that each bears on the hull side a triangle reversed, a cartoon elephant, and a nickname beginning with 'Doo . . .'; 'Doodlebug' (right) and 'Dood-it' (left) are visible, and the former also seems to have a pin-up on a dark panel forward of the name.

November, while 2/5th Marines mopped up Japanese remaining in the 1/5th Marines' zone. Some 450 Japanese were killed, although most did escape, while Marine losses were about forty.

On 4 November other troops who had arrived as reinforcements pushed through the Division's lines westward. However, as they were moving forward, word reached General Vandegrift that Japanese troops had landed at Tetere, east of American positions. He therefore halted the advance, leaving some troops on the new perimeter and bringing the others back as a precaution.

Meanwhile, work on a second airfield began at Aola on the island's eastern side. It turned out the land there was too marshy for a strip, so the site was abandoned and the 2nd Raider Battalion, which landed on Guadalcanal in October, began a long, 150-mile hike back from there through Japanese lines along the Gavaga. The march finally ended when they reached American lines on 4 December. They killed 488 Japanese while on the way, losing only seventeen dead and eighteen wounded themselves.

In mid-November the Army's Americal Division had landed, and the Marines had to admit that the First Division was officially 'no longer capable of offensive operations.' The Division's final action report notes: 'The cumulative effect of long periods of fatigue and strain, endless labour by day and vigilance by night were aggravated to an alarming degree by the growing malarial rate.'

By 7 December 1942, the anniversary of the Japanese attack on Pearl Harbor, the last of the troops who had dealt the Japanese Empire its first stinging blow were evacuated, and General Vandegrift turned over his command to the Americal's commander. The general watched the last of the 5th Marines embark, '. . . some so weak they could scarcely climb the cargo nets draped over the sides of the fat transports. Two days later I walked to our small cemetery called Flanders Field to take my own farewell of the almost 700 officers and men of my command who died in this operation. I looked in silence on the rude crosses that bespoke valiant deeds by great men.'

The Division, by taking and holding Guadalcanal, had caused the Japanese to lose great numbers of men and equipment and had driven a wedge into their Pacific perimeter. A leading Japanese Navy planner said later, 'After Guadalcanal I knew we could not win the war. I did not think we would lose, but I knew we could not win.'

Cape Gloucester

The veterans of Guadalcanal landed in Australia, where they became part of that continent's defence forces. A Division officer watched them land. 'The men were ragged, still dirty, thin, anaemic, shallow, listless. Just about one out of every ten of them fell down, tumbling limply down the steep ladder on their backs, landing pitifully on the dock.'

The Division was camped near Melbourne where, with tender, loving care from both drill sergeants and local ladies, the men slowly recovered their physical and mental health.

In July 1943 a reconditioned First Division received their first directive for an operation against Cape Gloucester, New Britain. The operation had the purpose of taking a Japanese airfield there which threatened the flank of an Allied advance towards the Philippines. By 23 October the last of the Division's troops had left Melbourne for Milne Bay, New Guinea, where the men practised landing manoeuvres, using the new LSTs, LCIs, and LCTs.*

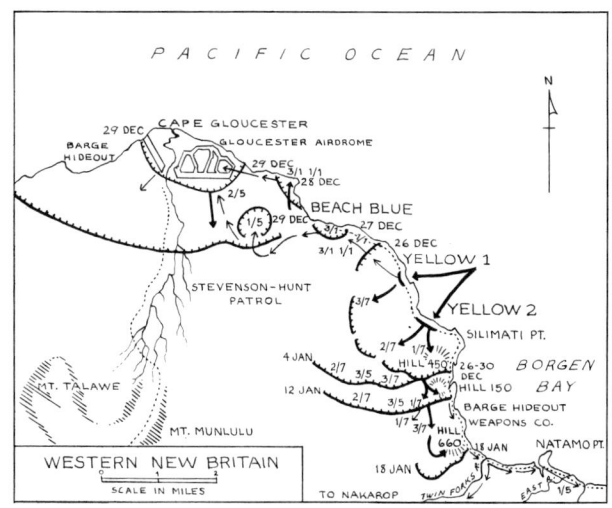

*Landing Craft

Many different models were built during the war. Some of the basic characteristics of major representative types are as follows:

Type LCM *Displacement* 22–52 tons *Dimensions* 50 × 14ft *Draught* $3\frac{1}{2}/4\frac{1}{2}$ft *Load* 1 × 30-ton tank or 60 troops.
Type LCV/P *Displacement* 8–11$\frac{1}{2}$ tons *Dimensions* 36 × 10$\frac{1}{2}$ft *Draught* $2\frac{1}{2}/3\frac{1}{2}$ft *Load* 1 × 3-ton truck or 36 troops.
Type LCI(L) *Displacement* 234–384 tons *Dimensions* 158$\frac{1}{2}$ × 23$\frac{1}{4}$ft *Draught* $4\frac{3}{4}/6\frac{1}{2}$ft *Load* 188 troops.
Type LCT5 *Displacement* 143–311 tons *Dimensions* 117$\frac{1}{2}$ × 32$\frac{2}{3}$ft *Draught* $3/4\frac{1}{2}$ft *Load* 3 × 50-ton or 4 × 40-ton or 5 × 30-ton tanks, or 9 × 3-ton trucks.
Type LCT7 *Displacement* 513–900 tons *dimensions* 203$\frac{1}{2}$ × 34$\frac{1}{4}$ ft *Draught* $3\frac{1}{2}/7$ ft *Load* 3 × 40-ton or 5 × 30-ton tanks plus 54 troops.
Type LCT2 *Displacement* 1065–2160 tons *Dimensions* 327$\frac{3}{4}$ × 50ft *Draught* $3/9\frac{1}{2}$ft *Load* 18 × 30-ton tanks or 1 × LCT5 or 27 × 3-ton trucks plus 8 jeeps plus 177 troops.

All had top speeds in the range 9–14 knots. Armament was light anti-aircraft only, the smaller types mounting a few machine guns and the larger types, 20mm cannon in addition.

At 3am on Christmas morning, 1943, the Division got under way for its second amphibious assault of the war. At 6am on 26 December the escorting cruisers and destroyers opened fire on the entrenched Japanese on Cape Gloucester. At 7.46am men of the 3/7th Marines were the first to hit the beaches, followed two minutes later by the 1/7th Marines. The 'beach' turned out to be a fringe of greenery overhanging the ocean, with a vast swamp just beyond.

The plan called for the 7th and 1st Marines to land and move quickly to seize the airfield, while the 2/1st made a diversionary landing at Tauali. The 5th Marines were in reserve. The landing worked perfectly; the 2/1st Marines were unopposed, and the other units met only light opposition. It wasn't until they got into the swampy jungle headed towards the airfield that they ran into a stiff Japanese defence. With the aid of some Sherman tanks, however, the Marines pushed the defenders aside, and all units were in their assigned phase lines by the end of 'D-Day'. Casualties among the Marines were only twenty-one killed and twenty-three wounded, with at least one of these crippled by a falling tree instead of enemy fire.

The weather became the big problem. It began raining by early afternoon on 'D-Day' and continued through the night, and then for five more days. The Division's after-action report stated: 'Water backed up in the swamps in the rear of the shore line, making them impassible for wheeled and

13

Part of the second wave of Marines landing at Cape Gloucester from their shallow-draught LCI, characteristically loaded with spare ammunition.

tracked vehicles. The many streams which emptied into the sea in the beachhead area became raging torrents. Some even changed course. Troops were soaked to the skin and their clothes never dried out during the entire operation.'

The second day's advance was slow. The few tanks that did manage to get up proved a decisive factor in breaking enemy defences. One tank platoon commander recalled turning a corner and running into a Japanese 75mm gun position. 'I saw one Jap walk calmly over and pull the lanyard. The shell—it was HE—hardly scratched the tank. They were so astonished they just stood there while we mowed 'em down and smashed the piece.'

A Japanese company attacked the 2/7th Marines at about 2.15pm on 27 December, but was easily driven off with the loss of 466 Japanese against a Marine cost of twenty-five killed and seventy-five wounded.

The 5th Marines were sent against the airfield from the south on 29 December while the 1st Marines moved on it from the east. Because of the appalling jungle, the 1/5th and 2/5th Marines were not in position until 3pm, and the attack began then. By 6pm the 1st Marines were on the airfield; the 2/5th Marines reached it by 7.30pm. On the evening of the 29th the Japanese launched a *banzai* charge on a narrow front held by the 2/1st Marines at Tauali. A single gunnery sergeant with a light machine gun broke up the attack, and the Japanese then spent the rest of the night trying to break through the battalion's lines in small groups. All were unsuccessful. At noon on 31 December the United States flag was raised over a completely secure Cape Gloucester airfield.

Once the airfield was taken, attention was drawn to three hills which dominate Borgen Bay: Hill 150, Hill 660 and Aogiri Ridge. Troops holding these hills dominate all of western New Britain. The 7th Marines, reinforced by the 3/5th Marines, were sent towards this high ground. On 5 January the battalions (from left, 1/7th, 2/7th, 3/7th and 3/5th Marines) set out in line through the swamps towards the hills which rose out of the green carpet. Combat correspondent Asa Bordages, with the 3/5th Marines, reported how that battalion came to a slightly wider, less green spot of swamp.

'The Marines didn't know the creek was a moat before an enemy strong point. They couldn't see that the heavy growth across the creek was salted with pillboxes—machine-gun emplacements armoured with dirt and logs, some of them dug several stories deep, all carefully spotted so they could sweep the slope and both banks of the stream with interlacing fire.'

The Marines tried to get across the creek under covering fire. Private First Class Calvin B. King's platoon actually crossed the stream four times that day, only to fall back each time under smashing fire. Only on the last occasion did they actually see a single enemy soldier. 'They were just coming at us through the trees. We were firing,' he said later, 'but they kept coming at us. There were too many of them to stop. We had to pull out. Machine guns were shooting at us from everywhere. And all them Japs coming. We'd pull back a little way and stop and fire, and then we'd fall back a little more.' Not one crossing was successful.

All night long the Japanese directed their dive-bombers on to the pinned-down Marines with their tracer fire. On the morning of 3 January the Japanese brought mortars into use. The Marines tried once again to cross that bloody stream, and again they failed. Snipers cut down survivors as they tried to get back across the stream. One party was forced under a bank, neck-deep in water, while one of their platoon lay across a log in plain view of both them and the Japanese. He'd been hit at least twenty times by machine-gun fire; he was still alive, calling, ever weaker, 'Here I am, Wills, over here, I'm here!' It would have been certain death to have gone after him, and the men stayed where they were while his blood, and the blood of others, flowed around their faces. Later they said that it was harder to stay there, doing nothing and listening to him, than anything else in the campaign.

Finally the Sherman tanks came up. The creek banks, too steep for them to traverse, stopped them. An unarmoured bulldozer, the driver sitting naked to enemy fire, then appeared. Corporal John E. Capito drove the 'cat' pushing three loads from the bank into the stream before being shot in the face. Staff Sergeant Keary Lane and Private First Class Randall Johnson crawled to the machine and, using an axe handle to work the levers, got it working again. Then Sergeant Lane got into the driver's seat and began smoothing out the banks again. He, too, was soon hit, but continued working until nightfall. By then the banks were level enough

Marines warily follow Sherman tanks which blast Japanese bunkers out of their path on the advance from the beach to Cape Gloucester airfield.

Marines in action at Cape Gloucester; note Thompson gun and pouches, grenades hooked to equipment, and fixed bayonets. In the larger photo, immediately below the second bogie of the Sherman, a dog can be seen; this beast became quite famous, as he led the advance all day, barking without pause!

for three Shermans to work their way across the creek and destroy two enemy bunkers. By 4 January both 3/5th and 3/7th Marines were across 'Suicide Creek.' Then the whole force halted to reorganize.

Meanwhile, back at Target Hill, which had been captured the first day, at 5.40am on 3 January the Japanese launched a two-hour-long *banzai* charge which was beaten off easily. Marine deaths were three; Japanese losses were over 200.

On 6 January, in driving rain, the forward movement was resumed. Co. 'A', 1/7th Marines, quickly ran into a stiff fire fight. Another bulldozer, whose driver seemed to have a charmed life, levelled stream banks and several Shermans crossed and drove out the enemy, capturing three 37mm guns and five machine guns. At the same time the 1/7th Marines took Hill 150, finding few defenders, and the 3/5th Marines went on to Aogiri Ridge, running into a position of some thirty-seven interlocking bunkers which the Japanese planned to hold at all costs. The Marines were stopped flat.

Lieutenant-Colonel Lewis Walt, 3/5th Marines commander, was just about everywhere at once, urging and encouraging his men. Once he joined the crew of a 37mm cannon, helping manhandle it into position and watching as it fired cannister rounds into the dense rain forest of trees, vines, shrubbery and pillboxes. Still the Japanese position held.

At about 1.30am on 10 January the Japanese, as they were so helpfully wont to do, leapt out of their well-built bunkers and, screaming, charged the Marines with swords and bayonets. This was just what Colonel Walt figured they might do, and his men were ready. A sheet of fire met the Japanese, who charged into that certain death five times. The colonel had one anxious moment when between the fourth and fifth charges his most important machine gun ran out of ammunition. It was a race between the ammunition party and the Japanese to reach the gun first. The Marines won. With that the back of the Aogiri defence was broken.

An attack on the 1/7th Marines the same night was easily turned back. By noon on 11 January the main Japanese supply and bivouac areas around Borgen Bay had been captured. Aogiri Ridge was later nicknamed 'Walt's Ridge' by the Marines.

On 12 January scouts reconnoitred the last bastion, Hill 660, which was defended by the Japanese 2/141st Infantry Regiment. The 2/7th Marines then dug in on the right flank of the Borgen Bay task force. The fatigued and bloodied 3/5th Marines were held back to rest while the 3/7th Marines were sent directly up Hill 660 at 6.50am on 13 January. A force made up of a half-track, two light tanks, a jeep, several 37mm guns, a bulldozer and some specialized troops were sent to support the battalion. According to the official report: 'Preceded by a heavy artillery preparation, the 3rd Battalion, 7th Marines advanced rapidly in column of companies to the northern slope of Hill 660 and at 0930 started up its slopes.'

It really wasn't that easy. One private in the attack recalled: 'You could hardly walk. If you'd try to watch where you were stepping, the vines would cut your face. A Jap sniper hit my buddy in the hip. I waited till he fired again, found him in a tree, and let him have it. I shot five times, and he dangled. He was tied in the tree. A BAR man sprayed the Jap and he came bouncing down through the limbs of the trees.' The Marines were stopped and, under covering artillery fire, withdrew.

The next day troops were sent around to the south side, where they found few enemy troops. Even though it was late in the day they pushed on up. A combat correspondent with them wrote, 'Our boys were tired, wet to the skin, and going on nerve alone. Not even Colonel Buse could explain it, but spontaneously those bedraggled and bedevilled Marines rose and charged that vertical face of rock and clay. They had been broken into small units by casualties and terrain and enemy fire, but these small units just kept going. That night we camped on the crest of Hill 660.'

The 3rd Battalion spent the morning of 15 January mopping up the slopes. The last fighting here broke out at about 5.30am on 16 January, when two Japanese companies staged a typical *banzai* charge, suffering a typical defeat.

When the fighting was over around Borgen Bay, the Division was sent some sixty miles east along the New Britain coast. The 5th Marines led the way, being held up for five days until 25 January by Japanese rearguards at the Natamo River before getting across. By 21 February the Marines had taken Karai-ai, some thirty miles east of Borgen Bay. By 8pm on 25 February the 5th Marines' command post was installed at Iboki, the end of the Division's long march.

On 5 March the 5th Marines were loaded into a motley naval convoy which then headed towards Talasea, a small island on the eastern side of the Willaumex Peninsula, some fifty-seven miles from Iboki. The only air support the Marines enjoyed was from a Piper Cub, whose pilot dropped eight hand grenades on beachhead positions, while 'naval' gun fire was supplied by tanks firing from LCMs! The 1st and 2nd Battalions landed successfully by 8.35am on 6 March, under a hail of Japanese mortar fire; this barrage landed in the midst of an artillery battery which was just being unloaded, but did not stop the infantry. The two battalions dug in just beyond the beach and awaited the 3/5th Marines, who did not get ashore until just before dark on 7 March. The next day the Marines pushed on towards the main Japanese positions on Mount Schleuchter. Under fire from mortars, artillery and small arms, the Marines succeeded in clearing the area by about 1pm on 9 March.

With New Britain secure the Navy wanted the Division back under its control, while the Army wanted it to stay in New Britain. The Navy finally won, and by 4 May the Division's last personnel boarded a ship bound for a rest camp in Pavuvu, the largest island of the Russells. The tired men were in no mood for the tiny, miserable, muddy, hot, poorly-equipped coconut-growing island; when they arrived, Pavuvu did not even boast any lights.

Lieutenant David M. Brown wrote home that on Pavuvu '... you have nothing much to think about except the details of daily routine. The prospect of a bottle of beer is a matter of interest and speculation to us here. One lad wrote in his letter of the things he bought at a recently opened PX [post exchange]—ink and a comb and handkerchiefs and shoelaces, chewing gum and a towel you could get at the meanest ten-cent store. "They are beautiful!" he says. And they are—as fascinating and novel as Robinson Crusoe's carpenter chest.'

One good thing about the spell on Pavuvu was that many of the veterans who had been with the Division from the beginning were rotated home—260 officers and 4,600 enlisted men. They were sent off by ship, the Division's band playing as they embarked. After a variety of popular songs, the band started up the Marine Corps hymn, 'From the Halls of Montezuma.' Many veterans wept.

Peleliu

Replacements, many of whom were the first draftees in Marine Corps history, had to be trained. The Division returned to the practice manoeuvre field. All the signs of another campaign were in the air.

Newly arrived 'cast hull' M4A1 Shermans move off Cape Gloucester beach and into the jungle; December 1943.

Artillerymen in camouflage-printed one-piece combat fatigues and round Marine fatigue hats fire their 75mm pack howitzer at Japanese positions near Cape Gloucester airfield.

The target was the Palau Islands, some 470 miles east of Mindanao in the Philippines: another flank to be secured as part of General MacArthur's overall plan for the drive back to those islands. Two islands were the targets. Angaur would be taken by the Army's untried 81st Division, while the First Marine Division would take Peleliu. This ocean speck, some six miles long and two miles wide, was expected to fall in what divisional commander Major-General William H. Rupertus said would be '. . . a quickie. Rough but fast. We'll be through in three days.'

Japanese documents captured on Saipan indicated that Peleliu's garrison totalled some 10,000 men. A coral reef lay some 500 yards off the beaches, so large landing craft could not get close enough to shore for the men to land directly off them. Everyone who made a combat landing on Peleliu would have to ride in on an amphibian tractor, the 'Amtrac'. Since Amtracs could not be launched as far from shore as the 18,000 yards that ocean-going transports needed to keep them safely out of enemy artillery range, the men would have to disembark first from the transports into LSTs. Then, after a short ride, they would get out of the LSTs and into Amtracs for the final leg of the assault. An LST could carry no more than a company at a time, so the assault would have to be rather piece-meal. The goal was to get 4,500 Marines on Peleliu's beach in the first nineteen minutes of landing. It would take considerably longer for all the 28,484 men in the reinforced First Division to land.

Peleliu's 10,700-man Japanese garrison came largely from the Army's élite 14th Division, with Imperial Navy support. The commander was Colonel Kunio Nakagawa, an excellent tactician. He had built a fantastic array of bunkers and

19

interconnected pillboxes, some as many as six stories deep, made with steel doors and gunports which commanded the whole island. His philosophy was to avoid the *banzai* charges which marked the defence of so many Japanese positions, usually disastrously. Instead he would let the Americans land and come to his positions in the mountains. As often happened, Japanese engineering skills were so much in evidence that naval gunfire from five battleships, eight cruisers and twenty-one destroyers failed to do any noticeable damage to the fortifications.

The plan was for the three regiments to land in line on the beaches next to the airfield. The 1st Marines would head directly across the airfield, the 7th Marines would turn south towards the waiting Japanese, and the 5th Marines would drive north against Japanese dug in on a ridge line. If this plan were to work the Marines would have to meet only token opposition. 'If the initial momentum of the assault did not overrun the rugged ground inland from the beach, the landing force would have been placed in a very difficult situation', the senior Division staff officers later wrote. 'The artillery would have possessed no suitable position areas from which to support the attack; the tanks would have had limited scope for employment; and logistical support over beaches commanded at short range by enemy weapons would have been extremely difficult.

'This course of action with 100 per cent successful execution would have been excellent; with less than 100 per cent execution was dangerous. Experience indicates that the rapid execution of this course of action would have been problematical.' (This masterpiece of tortured jargon may be translated thus: 'If the plan succeeds completely, we'll be OK; if it is less than 100 per cent successful, we're in bad trouble; and frankly, our chances are poor to nil.')

'D-Day' was 15 September 1944. It was a dark, grey day. 'For an hour we ploughed toward the beach, the sun above us coming down through the overcast like a silver burning ball', wrote artist Tom Lea, who made the landing there. 'Peleliu was veiled with the smoke of our shelling. New hits against that veil made brown and grey pillars like graceful ghost-trees by Claude Lorrain.

'Suddenly I was completely alone. Each man drew into himself when he ran down that ramp, into that flame. Those Marines flattened in the sand on that beach were dark and huddled like wet rats in death as I threw my body down among them. There was a rattle and roar under my helmet while I undid the chin strap and smelled the flaming oil and popping ammunition from the burning LVTs around us. Men of the first wave had penetrated about twenty-five yards inland as I looked up the sandy slope.'

Within a half hour General Rupertus learned that the island's capture might not be quick, but it would certainly be rough. One observation plane reported some twenty Amtracs burning off one beach and eighteen off another. One of the Amtracs which was hit was the 1st Marines' command vehicle. Communications were lost between Division and regiment, making the left flank the weak point of the assault.

By the afternoon it was obvious that the attack was stalled. The divisional reserve, the 2/7th Marines, were ordered in. Without enough Amtracs, it was a slow job landing the battalion on beaches still under fire. The sun had burned away the overcast and turned the island's beaches into one huge sizzling frying pan. About 4pm, in anticipation of the expected Japanese counter-attack, the men were ordered to dig in wherever they were. Most had not got nearly as far as originally planned. Inevitably, a counter-attack did hit the invaders; it was described by a wounded corporal in the 2/1st Marines:

'At 1715 someone shouted, "Here they come!" We knew it meant the Japs and not the water wagon. I pushed down deeper in my foxhole; rifle ready, I looked out over the airfield. From behind a bombed-down hangar I saw a cloud of dust with the ugly snout of a Nippon tank at the head of it, then came another, then another from behind a bunker, another from here and one from there. Sure enough they are coming. Jap tanks pouring out of their hiding places, dodging and swirling crazily about. All of us open fire with machine guns, automatic rifles, small arms, bazookas, or whatever we have. The Japs don't give up, they keep coming and coming fast, very close now. Things happened so fast from here on in with these tanks that I want to tell you about only what happened within ten yards of me.

Above: Landing craft away—heading for the shell-torn beaches of Peleliu.
Below: Holding the line against counter-attacks at Cape Gloucester, these Marines are armed with (top to bottom) the M1 .30 cal. carbine, the Browning M1917 water-cooled .30 cal. machine gun, and an M1928 Thompson sub-machine gun.

'D-Day' at Peleliu—Marines take cover behind a DUKW on the fire-swept beach, while one of many 'Amtracs' lost that day burns in the background.

'A tank rushed for the machine gun on my right, "Stoney" stands up in the foxhole (he's a lad with guts) and lets go a burst of automatic fire. The tank was not ten foot away when it burst into flame, leaving a trailing fire as it still rolled forward. The lower half of a twisted and burnt Jap body fell not a pace from me. The Marine machine gunners jumped to safety just in time as the tank came crushing over their nest, smashing the weapon to bits; still it rolled on, ran over the foxhole of "Chick" . . . "Chick" came crawling out as the tanks moved on, with only singed eyebrows. The Shambows' tank gave a final lunge as it blew up about ten yards behind our lines. Don . . . rushed up to give the tank a squirt with his flame-thrower, but only to meet a quick death as the turret gun spoke, catching him directly in the chest. One Jap raised his head above the turret to have a look at the situation. He found out the situation all right, and fell back into the tank only to be pushed out again by other Japs inside and to fall down alongside of his machine. In the bottom of these tanks is an escape hatch; one Jap rushing out of this hatch met instant death. Still another Jap inside raised a bloody and dirty white rag, and got his hand shot off. Then hand grenades were tossed into the tank.'

The light tanks were stopped by small arms and a few Shermans which had survived the landing. The attack had hit the wrong troops. Had the tanks hit the hard-pressed 2/1st Marines they might have destroyed the landing.

All night the Japanese kept up their fire, yelling through megaphones, 'Amelicans, Amelicans, pigs, dogs, Amelican pigs and dogs, you die, you die, you die!'

'Come on in and see what we did to your tanks!' a Marine yelled back. 'We're using them to pack fish in.'

At night the 1st Marines totalled up their casualties and found some five hundred men had been hit, about a sixth of the whole regiment. Reinforcements were pulled in from beach and service parties.

The next morning the attack got under way again. The 7th Marines were to take the high ground, while the 5th crossed the airfield and the 1st took the ground already nicknamed 'Bloody Nose Ridge'. The 7th Marines had the toughest fight ahead of them, but by the end of the day they had pushed the Japanese back enough to allow artillery to land and join the fight. The 1st Marines also faced tough resistance. The left flank was pinned, but the right continued to move forward despite heavy losses. Over the two days the 1st Marines lost 33 per cent of their men. The 5th Marines had things a bit easier crossing the airfield.

That night found the Japanese again bothering the dug-in Marines. Captain George Hunt's Company 'K' was one of those hit:

'The battle broke with a tremendous, angry roar as though a fiendish blast had shattered the doors of hell and exposed to human ears the horrible turmoil which bawled and writhed within. At the one hoarse cry, "There they are! They're comin' in on us!" the entire line opened up simultaneously, bursting into an uncontrolled din that stirred the most furious, savage instincts of a man. I found myself bellowing until I thought my lungs would crack—"Give 'em hell! Kill every one of the bastards!"

'The Japs were answering with grenades and mortars and rifles. Again I heard the whirring of shrapnel and the whine of bullets, many of which

The shallow lagoon enclosed by the reef 500 yards out from Peleliu beach was a handicap; here, Marines manhandle drums of fuel and water across the lagoon, while landing ships stand in outside the reef.

were smacking into the rocks, ricocheting and burning crazy trails in the air. The Japs were assaulting us with stampeding fury, wave after wave, charging blindly into our lines and the hail of bullets and shrapnel which we poured into them. Above the uproar I heard their devilish screams, "*Banzai, banzai!*"'

Similar attacks on other sectors were beaten off, while some of the Marine positions were subjected to mortar and sniper fire only.

On the 17th the 7th Marines moved ahead steadily. That morning the 1st Marines, their battered battalions lined up from west to east in the sequence 3rd, 1st and 2nd, pushed forward against 'Bloody Nose Ridge'. The 2nd was stopped on Hill 200 but, supported by artillery, pressed on regardless of great losses. The 1st moved ahead amazingly easily for an hour until it ran into a concrete blockhouse the size of a small block of flats. Some twelve pillboxes supported the position. Fire from the 14-inch guns of the USS *Mississippi* was called down, but the sturdy building still stood. Under cover of the naval fire, however, the Marines bypassed the position.

Concentrated Japanese fire forced both the 1st and 2nd Battalions to keep up the impetus of their attack rather than stop and reorganize. Using Sherman tanks, bazookas and flame-throwers, the 1st Battalion pressed on, ending up on the forward slopes of the first line of hills by evening. The 3rd Battalion, meeting less resistance than the other two, had advanced nearly 700 yards by nightfall. Losses were shocking. Private Russell Davis, with the 1st Marines, recalled reaching the cliff:

'We had lost heavily, ever since the beach, but I had not realized how bad the losses were until our companies moved out on the cliff. Clawing and crawling up the cliff went platoons that were no more than squads, and companies that were no more than large platoons. I counted one platoon. It mustered eighteen men on that push. But they went up.'

That night the Japanese attacked again, hitting the line between the 1st and 2nd Battalions. There simply weren't enough men to stop them. Quickly, Division sent the 2/7th Marines' Co. 'F' to plug the gap, followed the next morning by that battalion's Co. 'E'. The line held, but just barely.

On the fourth day, 18 September, some 115 pioneers, the last of the reserve, were sent to the battered 1st Marines. Survivors of the 1/1st Marines were pulled out of line. The regiment's line was now made up of the 3/1st, 2/7th and 2/1st Marines. The line moved on, only to meet the heaviest artillery and mortar concentration of the entire campaign. At about noon, the 2/7th Marines finally had to pull back out of range. Company 'B', 1/1st Marines, was rushed to reinforce the hard-hit 2/1st Marines. Very little ground had been gained, but 1st Marines' losses totalled 1,500 men.

The 5th Marines were sent to occupy nearby islands, while the bulk of the 7th continued to mop up Japanese dug in to the south.

On the 19th, Colonel Puller's 1st Marines again rose from their foxholes and half-stumbled, half-staggered towards the waiting Japanese. On the left the 3/1st Marines advanced almost four hundred yards before coming under fire. In the centre, the 2/7th Marines slowly worked their way along to contact the 3/1st Marines. The right side of 'Bloody Nose Ridge' was hit by the 2/1st Marines, who gained some five hundred yards. Company 'A', 1/1st Marines, a total of fifty-six men left out of an authorized establishment of 235, passed through the 2/7th Marines against tough opposition. When Co. 'A' returned only six men were on their feet.

Company 'C', 1/1st Marines, was sent to join the 2/1st Marines and fought to the top of Hill 100. There they found themselves cut off and surrounded. The company's handful of men then fought off constant Japanese attacks. With their ammunition just about gone, they killed Japanese with rocks, ammunition boxes and bare fists. They even tossed some off the hill's steep sides. The company commander, Captain Everett P. Pope, received the Medal of Honor for the stand.

The sixth day, 20 September, dawned. The 1/1st and 2/1st Marines and the Division Reconnaissance Company were merged on the right, reinforced by some dozen machine guns manned by clerks, cooks and mechanics. With the dawn came the expected Japanese artillery fire which stopped the 1st Marines' advance. In the late afternoon the 1/7th and 3/7th Marines replaced the few survivors still standing from the 1/1st and 2/1st Marines.

The 3/1st Marines advanced a short distance on 21 September, while the other units were still stalled on the hills. Casualties for the 1st Marines totalled 1,749 men by nightfall on that day. On the 22nd, the 1/1st Marines survivors were sent to the 3/1st but, even so, the 1st Marines virtually ceased to exist as a useful organization.

By the end of a week it was obvious that the Peleliu campaign was going to need reassessment. The 81st Infantry Division from nearby Anguar was brought in as reinforcements. On 23 September, at about 2pm, the 81st's 321st Infantry Regiment relieved the 3/1st Marines. The Marines were given a three day 'rest' on the beach, and then those who were not badly wounded were sent up to other units as replacements—not a popular move, but losses everywhere were heavy and replacements nil.

The 7th Marines were ordered to take the 1st Marines' old objective. They began to look for an easier way into the Japanese position than the one Colonel Puller had tried. The 2/7th Marines went along the east coast, while the 1/7th Marines went along the west coast road. The 1/7th and 3/7th Marines then attacked from the north while the 2/7th Marines came in from the west.

On 4 October the 3/7th Marines went after a prominent hill, 'Baldy Ridge', taking three smaller hills first. From one of those hills, Co. 'L' was sent to take a fourth hill right under the ridge. They scaled the almost vertical sides, reaching the top without serious loss. Once there they found a cave which they sprayed with small arms fire. This noise attracted Japanese notice, and they opened fire on the Americans. The platoon leader died, wrote a combat correspondent with the men, when 'bullets tore him from his grip on the cliffside where he was trying to withdraw his men to safer positions, and he fell to his death on the ravine floor many feet below.' The men still on the hill were trapped. Under smoke grenade cover they tried to escape, many more dying in the process. Out of the forty-eight men who had climbed the hill, eleven survived.

On 6 October the 7th Marines were withdrawn. Their casualties were now of the same order as those suffered by the 1st Marines. It was the turn of the 5th Marines to be thrown against those terrible ridges.

The regiment, under Colonel Harold D. Harris,

A Guadalcanal, 1942

B Peleliu, 15 September 1944

C Okinawa, April 1945

D Okinawa, May 1945

was placed in a surprising position. The colonel chose lines somewhat back from the original ones, with his flanks resting on the beach. It looked to the Japanese like the start of a retreat, and that night they began a series of small attacks with artillery fire. The 5th held. On 25 September, eleven days after landing, the regiment attacked the hill commanding the northern part of Peleliu. The Japanese held firm so the regiment swirled around them like a stream around rocks.

As they bypassed the Japanese, still pushing north, the 5th came under fire from positions on the island of Ngesebus, only a few hundred yards away from Peleliu. The Japanese had turned a phosphate factory there into a blockhouse. Colonel Harris called in naval and artillery fire and sent a battalion to take that island and Kongauru and Murphy Islands, which it achieved by 28 September. Some Japanese remained on the north-western tip of Ngesebus, but their threat was minimal, and the 321st Infantry Regiment secured and garrisoned the island.

With the islets captured, the 5th Marines returned to what the Division's final report called '... a slow, slugging, yard-by-yard struggle to blast the enemy from his last remaining stronghold in the high ground.' They continued to dig out the Japanese, using combinations of tanks and infantry, flame-throwers and machine gunners, and hand grenades and submachine guns. On 12 October the 'assault phase' of the Peleliu campaign was declared over. At 3pm on 13 October, the 321st Infantry Regiment was ordered to replace the Division's remaining regiment, the 5th Marines, in the line. The 81st Infantry Division fought on. It was not until 25 November that Tokyo received word from Peleliu, 'All is over on Peleliu.'

The last Japanese to give up there were a group of twenty-six soldiers and sailors, led by a lieutenant, who did not surrender until 21 April 1947. The garrison had fought magnificently. It took some 1,589 rounds of ammunition of all sorts to kill each defender.

For the taking of Peleliu the First Marine Division was awarded the Presidential Unit Citation.

Okinawa

After Peleliu, the Division's survivors returned to Pavuvu, happy for once to see the place. Major-General Pedro Augusto del Valle, the previous 'Divarty' commander, was named to command the Division. After resting, training new recruits and generally binding its wounds, the Division headed off on 15 March 1945 for its last landing.

The target was Okinawa Shima, the largest of the Ryukyu Islands, only 325 miles south of Japan. The island had long been held by the Japanese. The garrison, commanded by Lieutenant-General Mitsuri Ushijima, included the 62nd Division deployed south and east of Okinawa's capital, Naha. To the north was the 24th Division. Between the divisions were scattered the 1st and 23rd Medium Artillery Regiments, the 7th Heavy Artillery Regiment and the 110th Heavy Artillery Battalion, as well as three machine-gun companies, four anti-aircraft battalions and various mortar, rocket and anti-tank troops. North of the 24th Division was the Bimbo Tai ('Have Nothing'), an organization of the 44th Independent Mixed Brigade.

The defence plan called for allowing the Americans to land, and then holding them north of Naha and the ancient capital of Shuri Castle. The terrain there was characterized by heavily wooded hills, deep ravines and many caves. The plan was designed to neutralize American firepower, especially that of tanks. General Ushijima told his officers that 'The enemy's power lies in his tanks. It has become obvious that our general battle against the American forces is a battle against their M-1 [sic] and M-4 tanks.' The only Japanese armour on Okinawa was the under-strength 24th Tank Regiment, with fourteen medium and thirteen light tanks.

The Americans planned to bring some 180,000 troops to the island; four divisions would land abreast. The First Marine Division was to land in the very centre between the airfields at Yontan and Kadena. They expected heavy losses. There was a sea wall behind the beach which the men would have to climb, and a slope slowly rose up behind that—perfect conditions for defence.

'D-Day', called 'L' or 'Love' Day in this

The 1st Marines move off Peleliu beach — the firing line is just beyond the smoke rising in the centre background. Others dig in on the crowded strip of crushed coral at the edge of the water. In the original print of this remarkable battle photo, more than seventy Marines can be counted.

operation, was 1 April 1945. A seven-day-long preliminary bombardment dropped 27,226 rounds of naval gunfire on Japanese positions. At 4.06am on 1 April, the signal 'Land the landing force' went out, and at 7am troops, covered by ten battleships, nine cruisers, twenty-three destroyers and 177 gunboats, disembarked into their barges. They headed the 4,000 yards to the beach. Aboard the ships, others waited tensely.

'What's happening in there son?', asked a doctor, of the only wounded man to arrive at his floating hospital a couple of hours after the landing began.

'Don't ask me, Doc,' said the Marine, who had lost a finger-tip in an accident. 'All I know is everybody's going in standing up.'

There was no Japanese opposition.

By 9.45 the 7th Marines were through the village of Sobe, their first priority objective, and the 5th Marines were more than a thousand yards inland. Two battalions of the 1st Marines and the 4/11th Marine Artillery, the Division's reserve, were ordered in, and the divisional command post was set up at Sobe at 4.30 that afternoon. The amazed Marines were ordered to dig in for the night. It truly had been a 'love day'.

The next morning the Division moved out at 7.15am, in cool weather and over beautiful countryside. Again they met no Japanese opposition. A puzzled General del Valle told reporters, 'I don't know where the Japs are, and I can't offer you any good reason why they let us come ashore so easily. We're pushing across the island as fast as we can move the men and equipment.' On the third day, just before noon, the Division Reconnaissance Company, riding jeeps, reached Okinawa's far shore. They were then ordered to scout the Katchin Peninsula, which they did, while the whole Division reached the island's further side by that evening. By 4 April the whole area assigned for the Division to capture, an area which it had been thought would take fifteen days to secure, was in American hands.

The Division settled into a routine of patrols while the Army's 7th, 96th and 27th Infantry Divisions were pushing south against the real Japanese line of defence. The Army's drive was slow, too slow, and casualties were heavy. On 24 April the Division was ordered to get ready to join them, and on 27th April it was sent to relieve the 27th Infantry Division.

On 30 April the Division, which had moved through the 27th Division's positions the day before, went into the attack. The 3/1st Marines, attempting to take Miyagusuku, were hit by concentrated small arms, mortar and artillery fire, and fell back to their start positions. A Japanese attack hit Co. 'K', 1st Marines. Mud had put all but two rifles in the company out of action, but the Marines beat the Japanese back with bayonets and clubbed rifles.

The next day the 1st Tank Battalion sent three gun and four flame tanks to support the 3/1st Marines in the second attempt on Miyagusuku. Some 300 gallons of napalm were laid on the village, and Co. 'L' then passed through it easily, followed by the rest of the battalion in early afternoon.

At 2am on 4 May, the 1/1st Marines (along with some armoured Amtracs from the 3rd Armored Amphibian Tractor Battalion) were in position along the beach south of Machinato airfield when they saw, in the dim moonlight, approaching barges. Flares were fired: it was a Japanese landing party. The Marines opened up with everything they had and the 2/7th Marines were alerted as a possible reserve in case of a breakthrough. By 4am the bulk of the Japanese 26th Shipping Engineers were dead or wounded. Among their bodies one Marine found a carrier pigeon in its cage. The bird was released with a note attached to its leg: 'We are returning your pigeon. Sorry we cannot return your demolition engineers.' The few survivors were routed out by a war dog platoon.

The Division faced the main Japanese line held by the 62nd Division; this ran along low coral ridges with Jichaku on the right, Hill Nan and Hill 60 in the centre, and Wilson's Ridge and Awacha Pocket on the left. Behind that lay another ridge and the town of Dakeshi. Further on there was a draw in front of Shuri, behind which were another town and ridge, both named Wana.

On 5 May the 1/5th Marines, supported by fifteen gun and two flame tanks, started working its way slowly through this maze of ridges and pillboxes. The typical firefight range was so short that grenades were the main weapons used. The Japanese 23rd Independent Infantry and 14th

Independent Machine Gun Battalion held their positions on the Awacha Pocket, while heavy rains on 7 May slowed American tanks to a crawl. Meanwhile the 1st Marines faced equally slow, bloody fighting for Hills Nan and 60. On 9 May the 2/1st Marines, supported by flame-throwing tanks, worked their way up those hills while the 1/1st Marines pressed eastward.

A Japanese 47mm anti-tank gun on Awacha was finally silenced on 10 May as the 2/5th Marines went up the north slopes of Wilson's Ridge and the 1/5th Marines up the west side. On 11 May Wilson's Ridge and Awacha were in American hands. Some twelve gun and three flame tanks joined in this final push, supporting the 1/5th Marines.

The battered 5th Marines were then allowed a short rest and were replaced in the line by the 7th Marines, just in time for the 3/7th to turn back, with support from four 'Divarty' battalions, a Japanese attack. As the Japanese fell back, 1/7th Marines passed through the 3rd Battalion's lines on their own attack. They were stopped almost immediately, and the call went out for tanks to come up. These tanks were not only used for offensive operations, but also as ambulances. A tank would drive astride a wounded man and pull him up to safety through the belly escape hatch. Wounded men were also carried on tank backs, the turrets serving as shields from enemy fire.

The attack went on. The 2/7th was at the foot of Dakeshi ridge by 11 May. The next morning the town of Dakeshi was attacked by 1/7th Marines. A platoon leader, riding on a flame-thrower tank, led the way, followed by another flame-thrower tank and a gun tank. Reaching a position overlooking Japanese emplacements, they halted and worked over the ground with 75mm guns, .30 calibre machine guns and flame-throwers. Then the tanks fell back and infantry came up to take the ground. By the night of 12 May the 7th Marines had secured Dakeshi's crest.

The next ridge line was Wana, held by the Japanese 62nd Division's 64th Brigade along with survivors of the 15th, 23rd and 273rd Independent Infantry Battalions, 14th Independent Machine Gun Battalion and 81st Field Anti-Aircraft Battalion. Company 'E', 7th Marines, first sent a platoon towards Wana Draw, where they were pinned down. At about 6pm, under smoke cover, the platoon pulled out, while the whole battalion pulled back to Dakeshi that night.

The 1/1st Marines relieved the tired 2/7th Marines during the night of 14–15 May. Once in position, they turned back three separate attacks, aided by naval gunfire, artillery and air support. The fighting had so weakened the regiment that the 1/1st was formed into a single company which was relieved by the 3/1st Marines on 17 May. This battalion attacked constantly for the next three days, but could only gain a small foothold on Wana Ridge.

The ridge's weak point appeared to be on its right, and the only way to break through would be by combined infantry-armour tactics; but heavy rains had mired down the armour, and the battle became a stalemate.

On 16 May a force of twelve M-4 Sherman tanks and four M-7 Priest tank destroyers joined the 5th Marines in attacking Hill 55, which guarded the way into Wana Draw. Colonel A. J. 'Jeb' Stuart, who commanded the 1st Tank Battalion, later described the grinding, non-stop advance:

'Tanks and flame tanks ranged out to positions up to eight hundred yards beyond our front lines systematically destroyed positions on forward and

A Marine squad in combat on 'Suicide Ridge'; in the centre, one throws a 'Molotov cocktail' which he has just lit from the burning brand held by the man behind him. The Marine on the right has the discharger for the M9A1 grenade fitted to his Garand, and a .45 cal. pistol holstered at his hip.

During the fierce fighting on Peleliu a wounded Marine, already labelled for the medics, is given a drink by a fully laden buddy.

reverse slopes within that distance by point-blank 75mm gunfire into cave interiors, and by flame attack. In addition, tanks destroyed in a similar fashion enemy direct fire positions on forward slopes for an additional 1,500 yards to the front beyond the farthest point of tank advance.

'In order to give the enemy no opportunity to reorganize and reinforce, two relays of tanks were necessary to permit rearming while maintaining a continuous attack. This "processing" then permitted the infantry to advance lines some five hundred yards with relatively light losses, using the neutralization support of preceding tanks and artillery. Especially important was the fact that the ground so gained by "processing" was tenable, and held. The procedure was then repeated in a zone extended farther to the front.'

By 20 May, Hill 55 had fallen. The 1st Marines continued their push on Wana, but the terrain and the mud prevented the repetition of tank-infantry 'processing'. Finally, on 23 May, the 1st Pioneer Battalion went forward to fire raw napalm over the crest to burn the Japanese out. Even then, enemy mortar and artillery fire fell among the 1st Marines. Still, vital positions were falling to the Americans. A Japanese staff officer later said that they realized that their forces would be cut off and destroyed where they were unless they fell back to another defensive line. 'Consequently,' he said, 'it was decided to retreat in accord with the Army policy of protracting the struggle as long as possible.'

On 26 May, Japanese troops were spotted retreating by alert air patrols, and two days later a patrol of the 1/5th Marines discovered Shuri had only a few defenders left. Quickly the whole battalion pushed forward, and Lieutenant-Colonel Richard P. Ross Jnr, 3/1st Marines, raised an American flag over Shuri Castle on 31 May.

The Division received a Presidential Unit Citation for the 'bitter siege' of Shuri. The First had paid for the citation in blood. Some 180 officers and 4,065 enlisted Marines from replacement battalions had to be sent into its ranks by the end of May.

The Division pushed on in June over rutted, muddy roads after the retreating Japanese. Some road surfaces were nothing more than 'mud soup', three feet deep. Vehicles were abandoned. Men at the front found it difficult to get enough to eat, since supplies could not be brought up. Some supplies were dropped by air. Major-General J. L. Bradley, commanding the Army's 96th Infantry Division, gave the Marines rations from Army supplies. The general noticed that the Marines '... were not equipped or organized for a protracted campaign. I was glad to assist in supply, air drops, and care of their wounded. They were fine comrades and co-operated to the fullest extent.'

One private of the 3/1st Marines said of 4 June, a day he spent in miserable, driving rain, deep in mud and under enemy fire, 'This day was probably the most miserable spent on Okinawa by men of this battalion.'

The 1st Marines, on the Division's left, ran into Japanese on Yuza Hill on 10 June. Charging through sloppy rice paddies, then across a stream and a railroad track, Co. 'C' lost 75 of its 175 men in this action alone—but by noon they were on Yuza.

On 11 June the 1st Marines took Hill 69. The Japanese counter-attacked, using novel tactics. A large band of Okinawans tried to enter Marine lines. It turned out that every fifth 'civilian' was a Japanese soldier. Suddenly they broke away from the real civilians and charged the Marines. Despite the confusion, the Marines killed every one of the Japanese.

The 7th Marines, on the right, passed through the villages of Dakiton, Hanja, and Zawa, reaching the coastal city of Itoman on 7 June, an advance of 10,000 yards in a week. With Itoman's capture, the Division had a port, which solved its supply problems. Then the 7th Marines ran into Japanese dug in on the ridge line just beyond Itoman, called Kunishi.

The attack on Kunishi was unusual in that it was one of the very few night attacks the Americans ever made during the Pacific War. At 3.30am on 12 June the 1/7th and 2/7th Marines attacked a totally surprised Japanese garrison, and quickly took possession of the crest. 'The situation,' General del Valle said later, 'was one of those tactical oddities of this peculiar warfare. We were *on* the ridge. The Japanese were *in* it, both on the forward and reverse slopes.'

Reinforcements could not get across the open canefield to aid the troops on the ridgehead, who were counter-attacked in the morning. A platoon was sent in on tanks, six men to a tank; the tanks later brought back the wounded. Other tanks brought up ammunition, water and plasma to the defenders. These tanks saw little actual fighting themselves. By 13 June the Marines were in control of the ridge, although some Japanese were still clinging to caves on both sides and would have to be rooted out. It was a cave-to-cave fight, with tanks bringing out the wounded. Some twenty-one tanks were destroyed or damaged in the fight around Kunishi. Artillery was also of great use in the fights, breaking up counter-attacks before they began. One battalion commander later said, 'If the tank-infantry team was the offensive weapon, our artillery was our best defence. Not since Guadalcanal had the average infantryman realized how important it was to him.'

The 2/5th Marines were sent in to take the eastern part of Kunishi. On the night of 7–8 June the 7th Marines on Kunishi were relieved by the 8th Marines, who had been attached to the Division. Taking the ridge had cost 1,150 casualties, but the back of organized Japanese resistance was broken.

Opposite: Peleliu, October 1944—another example of the extraordinary work of US combat photographers. With the smoke of combat rising in the left background, infantry and Shermans of the 1st Division move into 'The Horseshoe'. The small pond barely visible on the valley floor beyond the large sinkhole in the foreground was the only source of water for nearby Japanese dug into the hillsides; many were killed as they tried to creep down to fill their canteens after dark.

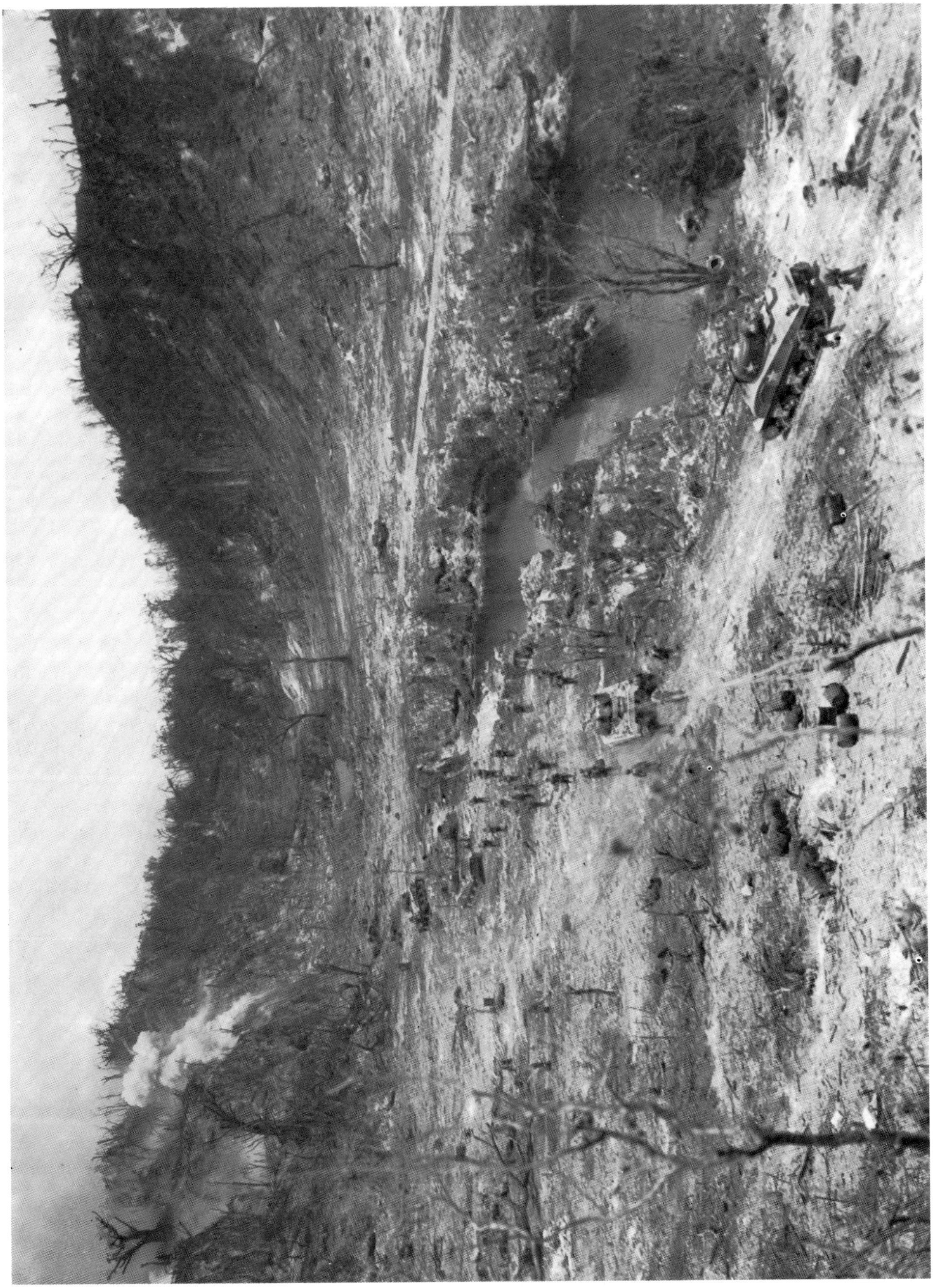

Okinawa, late March 1945—Marines make an astonishingly easy landing on the Jap-held island. Note that some wear fatigue caps beneath their helmets.

On 21 June General Ushijima and his chief of staff committed *seppuku*.* The Okinawa campaign, which cost the Division 1,115 killed, 6,745 wounded and 41 missing, was over.

On 27 May 1945, the Division began building its camp on the Motobu Peninsula, Okinawa. On 6 August the United States dropped an atomic bomb on Hiroshima. On 8 August the Soviet Union declared war on Japan. On 9 August the second atomic bomb was dropped on Nagasaki. On 10 August the Japanese offered to surrender. On 14 August the Japanese accepted the Allies' terms of surrender.

'A lot of us got drunk,' recalled one Division member of the day Japan surrendered, 'and ran around like chickens with our heads cut off; but I felt, and I think others felt, it was like doing what we were expected to do. Besides, it wasn't a very good place to celebrate. It seemed irreverent. It was only days before that your buddies had been dying. There were still lots of wounded men around in hospitals.'

* *Seppuku* = ritual suicide, usually but inaccurately termed *hara kiri* in the West.

On 26 September the Division embarked, not for home, but for another overseas tour. On 30 September the troops landed in Tanku, China, and the next day were in Tientsin, where a parade of honour was held for them. Elements of the Division were sent on to Peiping, while others stayed in Tientsin. The Division's job was to 'carry out the provisions of the surrender and to maintain law and order in the Tientsin, Tangshan and Chinwangtao area.' This tour, which brought them into almost constant brushes and 'incidents' with guerrillas, bandits and members of the Chinese Communist Army, lasted until they finally returned to the United States in October 1946. It had been a long war for the 'raggedy-ass Marines'.

The Division

Organization
Guadalcanal:
1st Marines, 5th Marines, 7th Marines, 2nd Marines (three battalions each), 11th Marines (Arty.) (four battalions), 1st Tank Bn., 1st Service

Bn., 1st Special Weapons Bn., 1st Pioneer Bn., 1st Engineer Bn., 1st Parachute Bn., 1st Amph. Trac. Bn., 1st Medical Bn., 1st Raider Bn., 3rd Defense Bn., Div. HQ Bn. Attached subsequently: 164th Inf. Rgt., US Army.

Cape Gloucester:
1st Marines, 5th Marines, 7th Marines (three battalions each), Div. HQ Bn., 1st Tank Bn., 1st Service Bn., 1st Motor Transport Bn., 1st Special Weapons Bn., 1st Amph. Trac. Bn., 1st Medical Bn., 17th Marines (Eng.) made up of the 1st Bn. (Eng.), 2nd Bn. (Pion.) and 19th Naval Cons. Bn., 12th Defense Bn., and 11th Marines (Arty.) (four battalions).

Peleliu:
1st Marines, 5th Marines, 7th Marines (three battalions each), Div. HQ Bn., 1st Tank Bn., 1st Service Bn., 1st Motor Transport Bn., 1st Pioneer Bn., 1st Engineer Bn., 1st Medical Bn., 11th Marines (Arty.) with four battalions, 3rd Amph. Trac. (A) Bn. (Prov.), 1st Amph. Trac. Bn., 6th Amph. Trac. Bn. (Prov.), 8th Amph. Trac. Bn., 3rd Bn. III Phibcorps Arty. (155mm), 8th Bn. III Phibcorps Arty. (155mm), 12th Anti-aircraft Bn., 33rd Naval Cons. Bn., 73rd Naval Cons. Bn., and 16th Field Depot.

Okinawa:
1st Marines, 5th Marines, 7th Marines (three battalions each), Div. HQ Bn., 1st Tank Bn., 1st Service Bn., 1st Motor Transport Bn., 1st Pioneer Bn., 1st Engineer Bn., 1st Medical Bn., 11th Marines (Arty.) (four battalions), 3rd Amph. Trac. (A) Bn., 1st Amph. Trac. Bn., 8th Amph. Trac. Bn., and 145th Naval Cons. Bn.

The Plates

A Guadalcanal, 1942

A patrol crosses the Ilu River; and one of its members settles down to the familiar chore of hunting leeches out of his pants and boots with a cigarette end. The Marines wear the two-piece fatigue suit of herringbone twill—the pattern accentuated in the foreground figure—in the shade known, like so many others, as Olive Drab. It appears from colour photographs to have been of every shade from dark green to pale grey-green, depending on age, wear and tear, etc. The only insignia is the black stencil Corps badge silhouette and 'USMC' on the pocket. Some NCOs painted chevrons on their sleeves, but for the most part combat fatigues were bare of rank markings. The usual long web gaiters were often abandoned, as they retained water inside the trouser-legs and boots after the frequent wading of streams and swamps. The fatigues were hot, and not as convenient for tropical combat as those issued by the Japanese. It was not for several years that orders were issued allowing divisional personnel to chop the trousers off above the knee.

The basic weapon on Guadalcanal was the bolt-action M1903 Springfield 30/06 illustrated here; its stopping power was superior to that of Japanese Arisakas, but it was not until the arrival of Army units with the M1 Garand that the superiority became very marked. The usual basic webbing equipment is worn here, the rifle belt supplemented by cotton and tape bandoliers. Often two water-bottles and two first-aid pouches were worn. The man on the left, taken from a photograph, appears to have a jury-rigged set of grenade pouches slung on his chest, apparently improvised from BAR magazine pouches. The combat-weary appearance

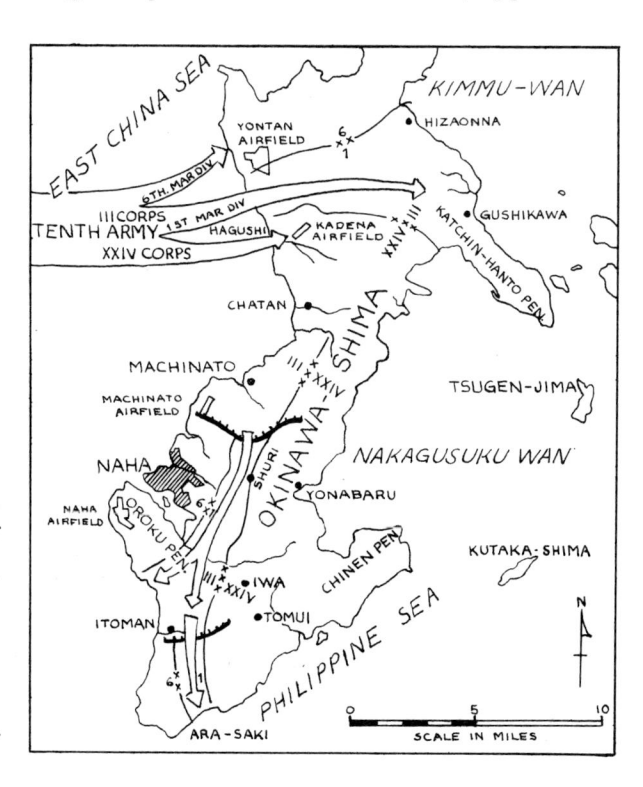

33

A 'composite hull' late-model M4 Sherman converted as a 'flame tank' lays a blazing carpet over Japanese-held ruins on the advance to Naha, capital of Okinawa, during May 1945. The practised collaboration of gun tanks, flame tanks and infantry was the key to the American advance.

of these soldiers is considerably played down from the reality shown by the eye-witness drawings of such artists as Donald L. Dickson.

B Peleliu, 15 September 1944

Peleliu was defended with vigour on 'D-Day'; here, under the cover of rocketing Corsairs, men of the Division prepare to fight their way off the beach and into the jungle. An 'Amtrac', its sinister nickname taken from a photograph of this action—'*The Bloody Trail*'—provides cover and supporting fire at the top of the beach; it is an LVT(A) 1, with the turret of an M3 Stuart tank. Behind it a red fluorescent cloth panel identifies friend from foe to the fighter-bombers. In the distance an LVCP lands men of the second wave. The Marines are dressed in the same twill fatigues as on Guadalcanal; they now have camouflage-printed helmet covers, and camouflage ponchos rolled on their packs. George McMillan recalled how, on Peleliu, 'to protect themselves against sunstroke, the men pulled out the cloth camouflage covers on their helmets and let it hang over the backs of their necks, so that they looked like Arabs.' Later, because of the heat, men discarded the helmets altogether, even in combat, and wore the 'old, soft, floppy fatigue caps of the Army', recalls Pvt. Russell Davis.

The man in the left foreground wears the waist belt of BAR pouches, and carries that weapon. The 'butcher' knife is typical. He wears his trousers loose over his gaiters. On the right are men armed with the .45 pistol, and the Thompson sub-machine gun of the same calibre: note the webbing magazine pouches for the latter. This heavy, slow, short-range man-stopper, a far better weapon than the unsatisfactory Reising sub-machine gun initially issued to the Marines, tended to draw 'friendly' fire in night fighting due to the similarity of its report to that of some Japanese weapons. All these assault troops still wear their knapsacks with entrenching shovels and ponchos.

C Okinawa, April 1945

Behind the front lines, a jeep carrying Japanese prisoners passes the emplacement of one of the 11th Marine Artillery's 155mm guns. It was on Okinawa that prisoners in significant numbers began to be taken for the first time—they were still enough of a novelty to attract the attention of the artillery sergeant in our scene. The correspondent Ernie Pyle was with the Division when two Japanese privates were discovered lying under some bushes, their hands over their ears, pretending to be asleep. Instead of fighting, the Japanese were '... so terrified that the marines had to go into the bushes, lift them by the shoulders, and throw them out into the open.' The Japanese uniforms show signs of considerable wear and tear by this stage. In practice, prisoners were often stripped to their loin-clothes by their captors, to be certain they had no concealed weapons or grenades. Parts of Japanese uniforms tended to end up adorning Marines. Pyle noticed how 1st Division men '... wore Japanese

Identifiable by its markings as tank 5 of Co. 'B', 713th Tank Bn., attached to the 7th Infantry Division of US 10th Army, this 'flame tank'—again, a 'composite hull' M4—supports Marine infantry on Okinawa. This is logical, since the 7th landed immediately south of the 1st Marine Division and advanced across the island on the Marines' right flank.

insignia or pieces of uniform. Later an order came out that any Marine caught wearing Jap clothing would be put on burial detail.'

The gun crew, taken from several photographs, wear a motley collection of clothing including the T-shirt in a strong green shade, camouflage-printed trousers, 'khaki' shirts—which colour photos show to have been a light yellowish shade—and OD clothing of all shades. The NCO wears the Marines' forest-green overseas cap. Pvt. Russell Davis recalls that '. . . the round hat was a favourite in the First Division. It could be bent into any shape, and serve against the rain or the sun.' The guard in the jeep carries the M1 .30 cal. carbine, popular and handy in tropical fighting, but lacking stopping-power. In the background are tents assembled from camouflaged shelter-quarters.

Note the yellow shade used for stencilling Marine serials on the sides of the jeep.

D Okinawa, May 1945

Marine infantry advance in the Naha sector, supported by a flame-tank of the Army's 713th Tank Battalion, attached to the 7th Infantry Division. This is a late-model 'composite hull' M4 Sherman; note the markings on the rear hull—'10A–713TK' and 'B5', and the painted-out star; the track extensions or 'duckbills'; and the appliqué side armour. Mixed units of gun and flame-tanks, working in close co-operation with the infantry, were the key to success on Okinawa.

The very motley appearance of the infantry in this mopping-up operation is taken from photos taken on the spot. The mixture of khaki and OD clothing of all shades; the hacked-short shirtsleeves,

Men of Co. 'A', 2/5th Marines in action on a ridge two miles north of Naha, which held up the advance for forty-eight hours.

Marines flush Okinawan civilians and Japanese troops out of cover in June 1945. Okinawa was the first battle in which any numbers of prisoners allowed themselves to be taken alive—though many still took the quick way out of what they saw as intolerable disgrace.

and green T-shirts; the use of the characteristic Marine fatigue cap underneath, or instead of the steel helmet; the stencilled name on the shirt back; the mixture of gaiters, and double-buckle combat boots—all are typical of the period. Weapons include (left) the M1 Garand fitted with the discharger for the M9A1 grenade, and (right) the M2 carbine, with its long banana magazine, which first began to appear in September 1944.

E Insignia

1, 2, 3 & 4 are the collar insignia of, respectively, officers of the Paymaster's Dept., the Adjutant & Inspector's Dept., and the Quartermaster's Dept.; and the Warrant Officer rank of Chief Marine Gunner. This latter wore a gold bar broken by a light blue stripe across the middle on each shoulder. Line officers wore the gold globe-and-anchor insignia on the collars of their dress uniforms. (Approx. half-size.) *5* is the globe-and-anchor Corps badge, here in the form worn on the blue dress cap of enlisted men. (Approx. full size.) *6* is the sleeve ranking of a Sergeant-Major, as worn on dress blues. *7* is the sleeve ranking of a Platoon Sergeant, as worn on forest-green service dress. *8* is the sleeve ranking of a Staff Sergeant, as worn on summer khakis. *9* is the sleeve ranking of a Master Technical Sergeant, as worn on dress blues. (All approx. half-size.) *10* is the 1st Division's shoulder patch, approximately full size. It was designed by the Division Operations Officer, Colonel Twining, on the plane bringing the Division's staff back from Guadalcanal; the stars represent the Southern Cross. The Colonel recalled:

'I bought a box of water colours, and turned in with malaria. I made six sketches, each with a different colour scheme. In a couple of days I went back to the General [Vandegrift] with my finished drawings. He studied them only a minute or so and then approved the one that is now the Division patch.'

The original patches were made by an Australian subsidiary of an American woven-name maker, and were first made available to the Division in February 1943, three weeks after the design was approved. Patches were worn on walking-out dress and overcoats. *11* is a half-size representation of the black Marine Corps pocket

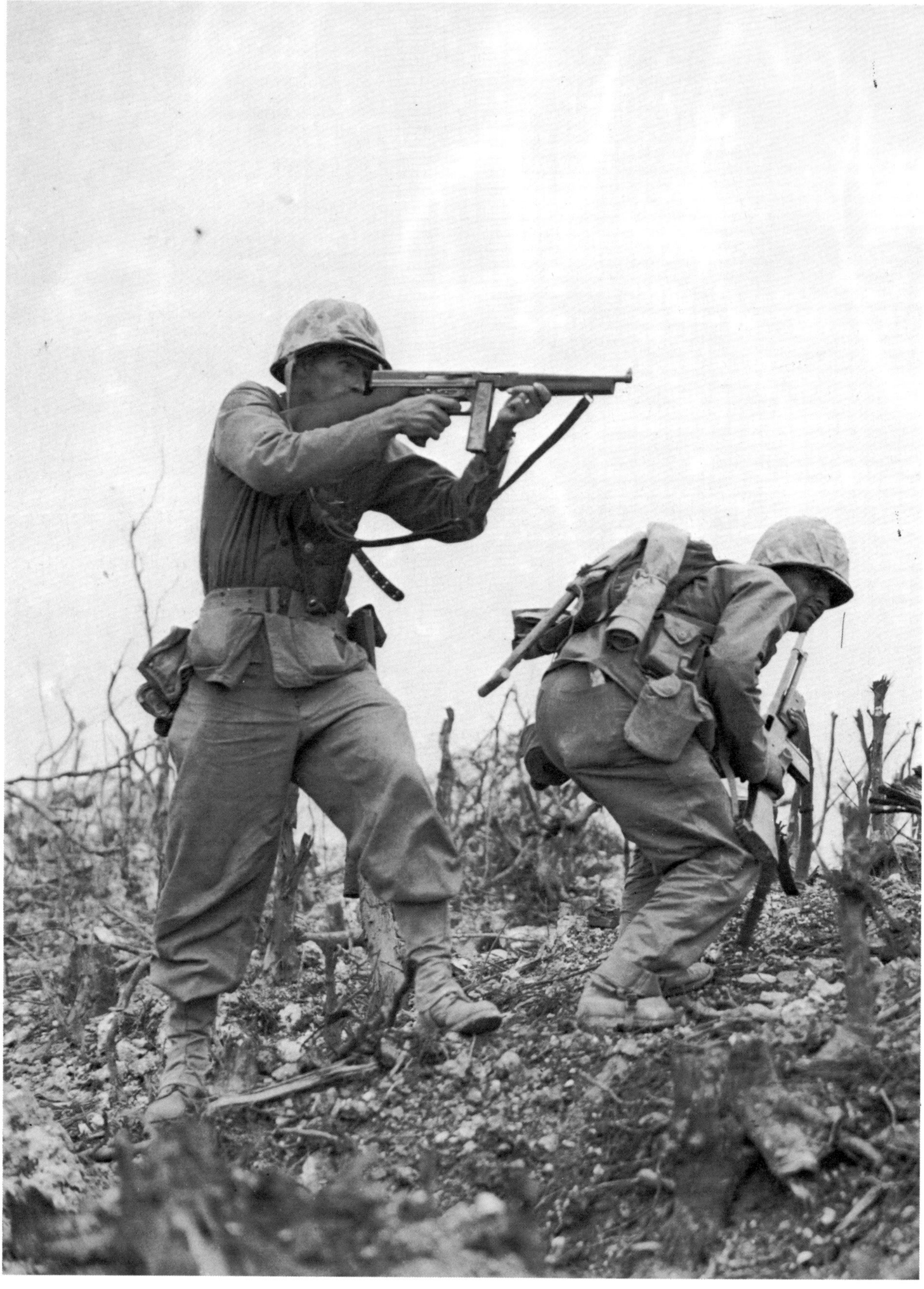

Left: A Tommy-gunner of the 1st Division aims his piece during a 'firefight' on Wana Ridge, near Shuri, in this classic photo of the Pacific War. Note the .45 pistol in a shoulder rig, for emergencies. **Above:** Flushing pockets of Japanese out of the coral caves. The top Marine has just thrown a smoke grenade over the rock, and it explodes in a shower of sparks as his buddies cover him with a rifle and a BAR. The man on the right has his name stencilled on his shirt back—'V. J. Murphy'.

stencil worn on OD combat fatigues. *12* is a half-size representation, taken from an actual example, of the printed camouflage pattern of the herringbone twill camouflaged combat fatigues used by some personnel of the Division. The same pattern was used for helmet covers and ponchos.

Finally, it should be noted that USMC officers' shoulder ranking was as follows: *2nd Lt.*, one gold bar; *1st Lt.*, one silver bar; *Capt.*, two silver bars; *Maj.*, gold oak-leaf; *Lt.-Col.*, silver oak-leaf; *Col.*, silver eagle; *Brig.-Gen.*, *Maj.-Gen.*, and *Lt.-Gen.*, one, two and three silver stars.

Select Bibliography

George McMillan, *The Old Breed*, Washington, DC, 1949

Major Charles S. Nichols Jnr, USMC, and Henry I. Shaw Jnr, *Okinawa, Victory in the Pacific*, Rutland, Vermont, 1956

S. E. Smith, *The United States Marine Corps in World War II*, New York, 1969

John Toland, *The Rising Sun*, New York, 1970

A. A. Vandegrift, *Once a Marine*, New York, 1964

Notes sur les planches en couleur

L'illustration sur la couverture montre des soldats appartenant à l'infanterie de la 1ère Division et un char M4A1 Sherman du 1st USMC Tank Battalion s'avançant vers le Cap Gloucester en décembre 1943.

A Guadalcanal, 1942 Une patrouille de 'cous de cuir' traverse la rivière Ilu; un d'entre eux se repose et cherche les sangsues qui se sont faufilées dans son pantalon et ses chaussures, les tuant à l'aide d'un bout de cigarette. Les soldats portent un treillis deux pièces en 'Olive Drab'—la couleur variait selon l'âge et l'usage entre un vert foncé, un marron jaunâtre et un vert gris pâle. L'arme typique à cette époque était le fusil à verrou M1903 Springfield 30/06. Le soldat à l'arrière-plan a façonné des poches porte-grenades à partir d'une cartouchière conçue pour le Browning Automatic Rifle.

B Peleliu, le 15 septembre 1944 Les hommes de la Division portent maintenant par dessus leur casque une housse en toile de camouflage; un certain nombre de soldats la glissent en arrière pour qu'elle serve de couvre-nuque. Les armes sont le BAR à gauche et le Thompson à droite. Un 'Amtrac' véhicule de débarquement amphibie LVT(A)1, ayant la tourelle d'un char M5 ouvre un tir de barrage en haut de la plage; son surnom est 'la traînée de sang'. Des chasseurs-bombardiers Corsair décrivent des cercles au-dessus de la tête des troupes qui indiquent leur position aux avions à l'aide de panneaux de tissu rouge.

C Okinawa, avril 1945 Une jeep transportant deux prisonniers japonais attire l'attention d'un sergent du 11th Marine Artillery Regiment dont le canon 155mm soutient l'avance de la Division; les prisonniers japonais étaient encore rares à cette époque. Les canonniers portent un mélange bariolé de vêtements en 'Olive Drab', et 'kaki', des vêtements de camouflage, des chapeaux de corvée et de soleil; le sous-officier porte le calot vert foncé appartenant à la tenue de campagne de l'USMC.

D Okinawa, mai 1945 Des soldats de l'infanterie de la Division, portant des éléments d'uniforme très variés, s'avancent vers Naha, soutenus par un char lance-flammes du 713th Tank Battalion de l'armée, qui était détaché à la 7th Infantry Division; notez les marques '10A-713TK' et 'B5'. Quelques-uns des soldats portent la casquette de corvée de l'USMC sous, ou au lieu de, leur casque; certains portent un 'T-shirt' vert au lieu d'une veste; d'autres portent des guêtres en toile à sangles et d'autres encore portent la chaussure de combat à deux boucles. Entre autres armes, ils avaient la grenade M9A1 qui était lancée à l'aide d'un dispositif lance-grenades fixé sur le fusil semi-automatique Garand (à gauche) et la carabine M2 à cartouchière en forme de banane qui a fait son apparition en septembre 1944.

E Insignes Les vestes bleues du grand uniforme porté par les officiers de l'infanterie de marine portaient sur le col l'insigne représentant un globe et une ancre, exception faite des officiers du Paymaster's Department (1), de l'Adjutant & Inspector's Department (2) et du Quartermaster's Department (3). Le sous-officier appelé Chief Marine Gunner portait l' 'obus' (4). L'insigne de l'USMC (5) était porté sur la casquette du grand uniforme bleu. Cet exemplaire est le type porté par les soldats engagés. (6) et (9) sont les chevrons de rang du Sergeant-Major et du Master Technical Sergeant et sont du type porté sur le grand uniforme. (7) est l'insigne de rang du Platoon Sergeant porté sur la tenue de campagne vert foncé et (8) est celui du Staff Sergeant porté sur l'uniforme 'kaki' d'été. (10) est l'insigne d'épaule de la 1ère Division porté sur la tenue de ville vert foncé et le manteau; cet insigne avait été conçu par le Colonel Twining après la campagne de Guadalcanal. (11) est l'insigne stencilé de l'USMC porté sur la poche des vêtements de combat et (12) est le dessin de camouflage imprimé sur quelques vêtements de combat et sur la housse du casque.

Farbtafeln

Auf der Titelseite abgebildet ist Infanterie der Ersten Division und der M4A1 Sherman Panzer des Ersten USMC Tank Battalion beim Vormarsch auf Kap Gloucester, Dezember 1943.

A Guadalcanal, 1942 Eine Spähtruppe von 'Seesoldaten' überqueren den Fluss Ilu; einer ruht sich aus, und verscheucht mit einer Zigarettenkippe Blutegel aus seinen Hosen und Stiefeln. Die Soldaten tragen zweiteilige Arbeitsanzüge aus 'Olive Drab' Körperstoff—die Farbe variiert je nach Alter und Abnutzung zwischen dunkelgrün, gelblichbraun und fadem grau-grün. Die übliche Waffen zu diesem Zeitpunkt war das M1903 Springfield 30/06 Gewehr mit Riegelfeder. Der Soldat im Hintergrund hat aus Mehrladetaschen für das Browning Automatic Rifle, eine Garnitur Patronentaschen für Handgranaten improvisiert.

B Peleliu, 15 September 1944 Die Männder der Division tragen nun Helme mit schutzgefärbten Bedeckungen—einige sind drübergezogen, so dass sie wie ein Sonnenschutz lose über dem Halsrücken hängen. Die Waffen sind das BAR (links) und das Thompson (rechts). Ein 'Amtrac'—ein LVT(A)1 amphibisches Landungsfahrzeug, mit dem Panzerturm eines M5 Panzers gibt Deckungsbeschuss am obersten Ende des Strandes; sein Spitzname ist 'Die blutige Fährte'. Corsair Jagdbomber kreisen droben, und die Truppen signalisieren mit roten Stofftafeln ihre Position zu den Flugzeugen.

C Okinawa, April 1945 Ein Jeep mit zwei japanischen Gefangenen zieht die Aufmerksamkeit eines Feldwebels, der 11th Marine Artillery Regiment, an, dessen 155mm Geschütz den Vormarsch der Division unterstützt; japanische Gefangene waren noch etwas Neues. Die Besatzung des Geschützes trug Bekleidung mit einer scheckigen Zusammenstellung von 'Olive Drab' und 'Khaki', getarnte Kleidung, Arbeits-und Sonnenhüte; der NCO trägt die dunkelgrüne Seitenmütze des Dienstanzugs der USMC.

D Okinawa, Mai 1945 Infanterie der Division, in zwanglosem Gemisch von Uniformen, rücken auf Naha vor, mit der Unterstützung eines Flammenwerfer-Panzers vom 713th Tank Battalion der Armee, welches der 7th Infantry Division angehörte; zu beachten wären die Markierungen '10A-713TK' und 'B5'. Einige der Infanterie tragen USMC Arbeitsmützen unter ihren Helmen oder an ihrer Stelle; einige tragen grüne 'T-shirts' anstatt Jacken; einige, Gurtbandgamaschen, und andere den doppelt-geschnallten Kampfstiefel. Zu den Waffen gehören die M9A1 Granate, die durch eine Entladungsvorrichtung im Garand Gewehr (links) abgefeuert wurde, und die M2 Karabiner mit seinem 'Bananen' Mehrlader, den es ab September 1944 gab.

E Abzeichen Die blauen Paradeanzüge der Marineoffiziere trugen das USMC Erdkugel-und-Anker Abzeichen am Kragen; ausser den Offizieren des Paymaster's Department (1), des Adjutant & Inspector's Department (2), und des Quartermaster's Department (3). Der Stabsfeldwebelrang des Chief Marine Gunner trug die 'Muschel' (4). Das USMC Abzeichen (5) trug man auf der Mütze der Paradeanzüge—hier, wie es von Unteroffizieren und Mannschaft getragen wurde. (6) und (9) sind die Dienstgrad abzeichen des Sergeant-Major und Master Technical Sergeant, wie man es auf der Paradeuniform trug. (7) ist das Rangabzeichen des Platoon Sergeant, wie es auf der dunkelgrünen Dienstuniform getragen wurde; und (8) ist das des Staff Sergeant, wie es auf der Sommer 'khaki' Uniform getragen wurde. (10) ist der Schultertuchstreifen der Ersten Division, wie man es auf der dunkelgrünen Ausgehuniform und auf Mänteln trug, nach dem Entwurf von Colonel Twining nach dem Guadalcanal Feldzug. (11) ist das schablonierte USMC Abzeichen wie man es auf der Kampfanzugstasche trug, und (12) ist das Tarnungsmuster, wie es auf einigen Kampfanzügen und Helmbedeckungen gedruckt ist.